ABOUT THIS GUIDE

When I first started my role at Child First as a State Clinical Director, I searched diligently for resources to help me support and guide affiliate site supervisors facilitating Reflective Group Supervision. While there was plenty of literature on group therapy, there was very little guidance on how to organize and conduct group supervision. I found myself adapting guidance from group therapy literature and drawing on my own experiences of supervision to support the site supervisors. Later, in my role as the director for the Center for Prevention and Early Trauma Treatment, I encountered the same challenge – trying to support consultants who were new to offering group consultation.

Thus, an idea was born: To fill this gap in the field by creating a guide for reflective group supervision. I reached out to Mary Claire Heffron and Deborrah Bremond as experts on the topic to inquire about their interest in putting something together. They enthusiastically agreed and went above and beyond in putting together a very practical and easy-to-read guide that is sure to become a favorite for professionals working with infants, young children, and their families.

You will notice that the Guide is divided into three sections, each dealing with an aspect of reflective group consultations. Throughout the document, you will also find many examples and suggestions for implementation. We recommend reading this guide in its entirely and then keeping it close by to refer back to as needed.

Luckily, there are now a few more resources available to the field. You can find those in the bibliography of this guide.

A note about the cover design: I recently read a novel about a young man's journey through life where each phase was marked by one of the elements: Earth, Water, Wind and Fire. It occurred to me that groups go through a similar journey, starting with getting to know each other and getting their feet on the ground, sometimes referred to in literature as the forming stage (**Earth**). Then groups typically encounter some turbulence and tension as members settle into their roles and become more comfortable with each other, referred to as Storming (**Wind**). This is followed by a period where the group establishes its norms, interactions are largely cordial and smooth, referred to in the literature as Norming (**Water**). Finally, the group is on **Fire**: they are a cohesive unit able to freely support and challenge each other; ruptures and repairs occur frequently and are understood to be part of the process. **Thank you to Grace Soliman for capturing this concept so elegantly with her original illustration.**

Salam Soliman, PsyD, IMH-E-Clinical Mentor
Director, Center for Prevention and Early Trauma Treatment
National Service Office for Nurse-Family Partnership and Child First

TABLE OF CONTENTS

ABOUT THE AUTHORS

DEBORRAH BREMOND, Ph.D, MPH

MARY CLAIRE HEFFRON, Ph.D

Deborrah Bremond has worked in the field of infant and early childhood mental health for the past 30 years. She has a broad range of experience conceptualizing, developing, and implementing integrated service delivery models for young children, birth to age 8, and their families. She has worked to integrate the importance of early social and emotional development into pre-school special education sites, neonatal follow-up programs, primary pediatric care settings, and community-based organizations serving families and young children. Dr. Bremond recently retired from her position as a senior mental health consultant in the Early Intervention Services program at UCSF Benioff Children's Hospital Oakland. She continues to consult and train Early Head Start and Child Care partners and work with the Substance Abuse Mental Health Administration grant for the Integration of mental health into Public Health/Maternal and Child Health through Alameda County's Project LAUNCH. Dr. Bremond received her doctorate from the Wright Institute in Clinical Psychology in 1992 and a Masters in Public Health from U.C. Berkeley in Maternal and Child Health. Dr. Bremond believes that our social safety network is challenged to develop blended funding models that embrace service integration and that focus on the continuum of family need from primary prevention to treatment.

Mary Claire Heffron is a psychologist with broad experience locally, nationally, and internationally in the infant, family, and early childhood field including clinical work, supervision, program development, consultation, professional training, teaching, and research. Her work crosses disciplines and she has a particular interest in the ways that group and individual reflective practice and supervision can support equity, diversity, and inclusion among staff and leaders, as well as trauma-informed care at the individual and organizational level. She has authored numerous publications aimed at practitioners and leaders who support early relational health and well-being and currently is on the faculty and leadership team of the Reflective Supervision Collaborative **https://www.swhd.org/ rsc/.** She also acts as a consultant and trainer with a variety of community mental health, child welfare, and training programs. Dr. Heffron is a former Fulbright Scholar and is medical staff emeritus at UCSF Benioff Children's Hospital Oakland.

NOTE FROM THE AUTHORS

It has been a pleasure and a challenge to develop this guide and we hope that reading it supports the work you are doing and inspires you to further explore the resources about groups that are included. We are grateful to our mentors and the many participants from groups we have facilitated who have helped us realize the power and potential of reflecting together.

INTRODUCTION

HOW THIS GUIDE IS ORGANIZED

This guide has three sections that detail the why and how of planning and running reflective practice groups of all kinds for programs serving infants, young children, and families. The guide is meant for administrators, leaders, planners, and reflective practice facilitators of these groups. It is intended for use across multiple systems, disciplines, and programs and includes materials and examples that address ways of using reflective practice that infuse a focus on race, equity, diversity, and inclusion. The guide is intended to provide information and resources for ongoing groups of various kinds that are a part of an agency's support infrastructure or that serve professional communities.

Each section contains information, quotes, vignettes, reflective questions and online resources to help illustrate the ideas presented. Online resources follow each section. A bibliography and resource section with sample materials are included.

Section 1 is an introduction that contains a short history and overview of reflective practice and the use of reflective practice groups as a tool for professional development, staff collaboration, support, planning, education, and other purposes. There is information on some of the research and evaluation studies that support the rationale for the use of reflective practice groups in all kinds of settings that provide intervention and services with a focus on relational health and well-being.

Section 2 is a planning guide for administrators, leaders, planners, and reflective practice group facilitators at the agency, community, and system level to plan, support, and evaluate reflective practice groups.

Section 3 is a detailed implementation guide for reflective practice group facilitators that includes guidance on structuring groups, connecting activities, grounding and mindfulness exercises, diversity- informed facilitation techniques, common challenges in groups, ruptures that can occur and pathways to repair. Within this guide we have incorporated reflective group practices and strategies from multiple sources, including the FAN (Facilitating Attuned Interaction) approach, and other materials related to reflective group functioning. These sources will be noted in the text and cited in the bibliography.

SECTION 1

INTRODUCTION TO REFLECTIVE PRACTICE GROUPS

"There is a high, hard ground overlooking a swamp. On the high ground, manageable problems lend themselves to solution through the use of research-based theory and technique. In the swampy lowlands, problems are messy and confusing and incapable of technical solution. The irony of this situation is that the problems of the high ground tend to be relatively unimportant to individuals or society at large, however great their technical interest may be, while in the swamp lay the problems of greatest human concern."

—Donald A Schon, Knowing in Action, 1983.

What Do We Mean by "Reflective Practice"?

Reflective practice is the way that work is done in the swamp, where meaning and a path forward are frequently obscured. While Schon's notable quote can seem to imply that the swamp is a treacherous place full of potential pitfalls, it is worth remembering that the swamp is also a place that teems with surprises, less obvious resources, and hidden beauty that can open possibilities for unique approaches that illuminate new perspectives and possibilities. In this swampy and often mysterious land where we do our work, the tools of reflective practice help us create possibilities for deeper collaboration, positive change, and healing.

As we think about reflective practice, it is helpful to consider the distinction between specific knowledge related to young children and families and what is needed to apply that knowledge in an intervention setting. A strong knowledge of child and family development, risk and resiliency, and relational health is foundational in any kind of infant and early childhood program. Knowledge based on the kind of work being done is also needed, whether these are the specifics of a particular model or approaches related to a specialty service area such as home visiting, infant mental health, child development and care centers, child welfare, occupational therapy, or speech therapy. While this knowledge is precious, alone, it is not sufficient for effective service delivery.

To intervene productively, providers from a variety of models and service areas must also be able to effectively engage with clients. To build effective programs and community projects, professionals must be able to collaborate effectively. These abilities are more than a set of techniques and include the capacity to reflect on one's own thinking and feelings as well as on that of others. The capacity to relate and engage effectively are supported by what is often referred to as reflective functioning (RF). Reflective functioning describes one's capacity to build an increasingly complex awareness that there is more going on than what is visible on the surface (Benbassat, 2020).

Fonagy (1991) stated that reflective functioning is dependent on the individual's ability to understand human behavior in terms of underlying mental states such as thoughts, feelings, desires, beliefs, and intentions. When a provider or professional of any kind approaches their work through this lens, there is often more appreciation for the social location, experiences, needs, and perspectives of others. Reflective functioning includes the use of critical self-reflection to examine one's own thoughts, feelings, biases, and physiological responses. It involves meaningful consideration of the perspectives of others to enrich and expand available information so one can more easily attune to others, grow understanding, suspend judgment, sustain empathy, and work collaboratively with clients. Reflective function slows down the tendency to quickly judge and move towards fixing or imposing one's idea of what is right. Rather, reflective function helps one lean towards a fuller realization of the feelings, dynamic processes, needs, historical context, and cultural differences involved in any situation. These elements are used in reflective practice groups to learn to approach dilemmas, and even impasses, in an open and curious manner that builds understanding and opens new possibilities.

Much of the particular knowledge needed to work with young children and parents can be acquired and updated over time through coursework or reading. However, learning the processes of how to intervene requires opportunities to think about, reflect, and explore ways to be with others that facilitate growth and healing. These capacities and approaches support providers to explore, grasp, tailor and apply approaches that are more likely to support change and growth. These same processes support trauma-informed care and the use of lenses that expand abilities to more fully consider racial understanding, diversity, equity, and inclusion.

Deepening the process of reflective functioning is enhanced both by participation in 1:1 supervision, and through reflective practice groups. These groups provide a fertile learning environment for participants to grow through their explorations with others. And, they also provide a fertile learning environment for participants to grow through interactions with others who may see the world through a different lens. Additionally, groups can also be a place where individual practitioners come together for replenishment, inspiration, and for finding or rediscovering a sense of purpose. Reflective practice groups can be spaces where providers can investigate their own experience of the work, feel held in their struggles and uncertainty, expand personal resources, experiment with new approaches, and experience an open space for new understanding to emerge that can be carried forward into their work.

Deepening and recharging reflective capacity is an ongoing personal and professional process that can occur through a group setting. Groups can create a sense of community where the participants are seen and validated. Some of the most salient outcomes of this process can be the reduction of the stress and strain of emotional labor that is often present in work with young children and families, an increase in compassion satisfaction, and higher rates of staff retention.

"The ability to make good decisions is a combination of experience and reflection,"
— Aristotle

A Very Brief and Incomplete Glimpse at the Long and Venerable History of Reflective Practice

Meditation and mindfulness are ancient practices believed to have originated several thousand years ago in India, spreading quickly throughout Asia. In more recent times meditation and mindfulness practices have been adopted and adapted to western cultures and many studies have catalogued the associated mental and physical health benefits. The study and use of reflection about oneself and others is noted within ancient texts from many traditions. Reflection is linked to perception and awareness of thoughts, feelings and sensations of self and others.

Many groups have integrated reflection into their philosophies of consciousness and have developed practices that embody this. For example, Native American traditions often include sitting in a circle where all participants can see one another. A special object, a talking piece, is passed and whoever is holding that piece has the sole right to speak and receive the full attention of others. In a circle everyone is equal; it is a non-hierarchical way of being with others to listen and learn. It combines ancient traditions with contemporary concepts of democracy and inclusivity (Pranis, 2005). Contemporary reflective practice groups utilize these principles of listening and learning from one another's perspective, experiences and skills. When groups meet in person, circular seating arrangements are commonly used to facilitate attentive listening. A variety of grounding and meditative practices, silence, and prayer are also commonly brought into groups to mark a transition into the working space of the group.

While reflection has been a valued activity in many cultures for a long expanse of time, more recently it has been intentionally used as a practice in many professions including mental health, social work, education, health, and business. In the early 20th century John Dewey, an educator, philosopher and psychologist, wrote *How We Think* (Dewey, 1910), which celebrated reflection and can be summarized in a quote from his work that states: "We do not learn from experience, we learn from reflecting on experience."

Donald A. Schon, a philosopher, wrote a series of books that centered on the use of reflection across disciplines. To sum up his work in his own words:

"The reflective practitioner allows [themself] to experience surprise, puzzlement, or confusion in a situation which [they] find uncertain or unique. [They] reflect on the phenomenon before [them] and on the prior understandings which have been implicit in [their] behavior. [They] carry out an experiment which serves to generate both a new understanding of the phenomenon and a change in the situation."
— (Schon, 1983).

Schon's work also stressed the importance of reflecting before returning to a particular situation. He also described thinking "in action" or the ability to be engaged with another and use reflective processes during such an interaction.

Caplan's (1970) Theory and Practice of Mental Health Consultation is a key publication that began to describe and advocate for a more client-centered and collaborative approach to consultation that focused on work dilemmas and advised mental health consultants not to probe beyond the work related concerns. He also advocated for work at all levels of an organization, including program managers and leaders, a practice that continues today in agencies receiving consultation.

Many other writers and practitioners have contributed to these reflective practices, such as Graham Gibbs (1988), who developed the Gibbs Reflective Cycle, now widely used particularly in educational settings, and writers such as Christopher Johns (2008), who wrote about the beneficial application of reflective practices in the nursing profession.

In 1992, Zero to Three, The National Center for Infants, Toddlers and Families, published *Learning Through Supervision and Mentorship to support the Development of Infants, Toddlers and Their Families: A Source Book*. It featured a series of seminal articles that set the stage for reflective practice and supervision practice in the infant and early childhood field. This classic continues to inspire and inform to this day. In this volume, editors Emily Fenichel and Linda Eggbeer described reflective practice, supervision and mentorship as relationships for learning, characterized by reflection, collaboration and regularity. This was followed by other practitioners who began to increase the use of these practices across the field and develop resources to support further development of reflective supervision and practices.

This guide is written in that tradition, with an emphasis on group reflective practices. We hope that the content of this guide inspires and supports others to develop approaches that meaningfully center diversity, equity, inclusion, and identity in their work.

While reflective practice and supervision have always included a focus on slowing down, reflective supervisors and consultants are now applying mindfulness and grounding techniques to promote presence, participation and dialogue. Jack Kornfield (1993) and Jon Kabat-Zinn (2010), both noted psychologists influenced by Buddhist traditions, describe reflection *as* mindfulness, as it requires a balanced, kind, non-judging attention that allows the individuals to free themselves from reactivity and to respond thoughtfully. Kabat-Zinn's work was one of the first interventions that showed how mindful reflective practices that increase self-understanding can also reduce the stress of medical providers (Shapiro, 2005).

> *"I have seen that in great undertaking , it is not enough for man to depend simply on himself."*
> — **Teton Sioux**

Resmaa Menakem (2017), a contemporary clinical trauma specialist and author, has written extensively about mindful approaches from the perspective of body-based awareness about racial trauma. In his description of somatic abolitionism, he recommends guided meditation exercises to help individuals deepen their capacity to think about racism through body awareness and use of mindfulness approaches that help build awareness and titrate the felt impact of oppressive racial experiences. He has also stated that it is only when we are in close proximity to others that we begin to intimately explore the boundaries of our virtues by slamming into our limitations. This statement underscores how reflective practice groups can promote professional growth related to race, difference, equity and inclusion by centering interactive group processes.

Mindfulness and reflective practice are also poised to address secondary traumatic stress (STS). This can be done through intentional focus and by exploring and supporting the experience of practitioners. The collaborative manner supported by Caplan (1970) is also inherent in exploring and regulating distress in reflective consultation while promoting perspective taking for the practitioner. Over time, research has contributed further to the evidence base of reflective practices in ameliorating STS. The National Child Traumatic Stress Network (NCTSN) has developed competencies and resources related to using reflective practices to reduce the secondary traumatic stress on professionals working with children and families. These links are in the Online Resources – Section 1 at the end of this section as well as in the Resources section at the end of this guide.

Increasingly the various disciplines serving infants, young children, and families link their theoretical stance on reflection to attachment theory and work that emphasizes reflective capacity as "the ability to think about the thoughts and feelings of self and other," (Fonagy,1991).

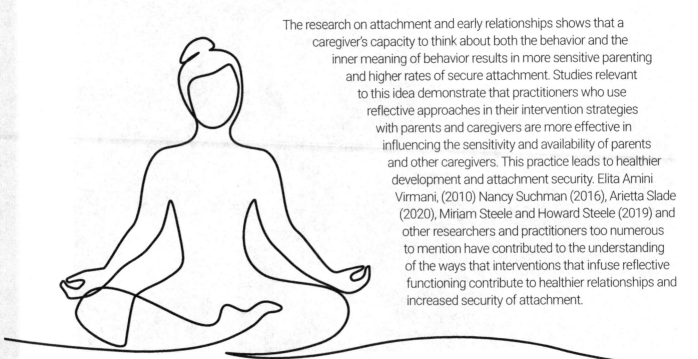

The research on attachment and early relationships shows that a caregiver's capacity to think about both the behavior and the inner meaning of behavior results in more sensitive parenting and higher rates of secure attachment. Studies relevant to this idea demonstrate that practitioners who use reflective approaches in their intervention strategies with parents and caregivers are more effective in influencing the sensitivity and availability of parents and other caregivers. This practice leads to healthier development and attachment security. Elita Amini Virmani, (2010) Nancy Suchman (2016), Arietta Slade (2020), Miriam Steele and Howard Steele (2019) and other researchers and practitioners too numerous to mention have contributed to the understanding of the ways that interventions that infuse reflective functioning contribute to healthier relationships and increased security of attachment.

The increasing awareness of the need to increase the diversity and cultural awareness of the infant and early childhood workforce has led to interest in the adaptation of reflective practices to advance these ideas and practices. (Clark et al., 2019; Lingras, K, 2022).

The practices we elaborate on in this guide are drawn from a variety of writers, theoreticians, and groups that explored reflective practice and the experiences of reflective practice facilitators and supervisors. We believe that staff deserve to receive reflective support about their work so that they are more aware of the impact of their own social location on others and better equipped to interact with their clients in ways that take account of each person's unique history, background, perspective, cultural lens, and aspirations.

"It is in collectivities that we find reservoirs of hope and optimism." **—Angela Davis**

The Importance of Group Reflective Practice

Deepening reflective functioning through reflective practice can happen alone, however, it is often hard to fully realize one's motivations, blind spots and limitations without the help of a benevolent other or others. Our focus in this guide is to describe and direct attention to the unique power of group reflective practice as an effective and essential space for learning about oneself and others, professional and personal growth, support, and developing a common sense of mission, professional identity and socio-cultural awareness.

William Bion (1961) a British psychologist who was well known for his study of groups, summarized that groups worked well when participants had an understanding of the group's purpose, a sense of presence, cooperation with each other, and attention to the group. Later Bruce Tuckman (1965) wrote about the stages of a group:

FORMING Learning About Each Other
STORMING Challenging Each Other
NORMING Working With Each Other
PERFORMING Working As One
ADJOURNING Celebrating And Reflecting

Irving Yalom and his colleagues continue to describe, research and write about the power of groups and contribute specifics about group formation, processes, and the role of group leaders. While the groups Yalom describes are used for a variety of therapeutic purposes in many different settings, his descriptions of group functions, dynamics, and facilitation have deeply informed our thinking about reflective practice groups used in diverse multidisciplinary settings and in a variety of infant and early childhood programs (Yalom and Leszcz, 2020).

Group reflective practice as described by these and other researchers and clinicians is a powerful form of learning, connection, and expansion. At times an active group becomes like one capacious mind holding and examining a confusing situation. In groups that function well, participants are reflective partners who listen deeply to one another, observe, and ask questions that extend learning and spotlight emergent perspectives. In a group that feels safe and inclusive, members can provide valuable insights to one another, notice and question a limited perspective or a microaggression, support each other as difficult material or broader understanding unfolds, and bear witness to the difficulty of tolerating the slow pace of change or the anger at the scarcity of needed resources. The group learning format also provides an avenue for experimenting with new skills and knowledge.

Additionally, individuals who are in groups together often extend this support to each other in their day- to-day work environments.

There are a variety of skills that are practiced in groups that have a direct application for any human service activity, such as listening and providing feedback, hearing another's perspective, examining a known phenomenon through a different cultural or racial lens, and negative capability which is the capacity to listen even though you might disagree, want to correct or offer an immediate solution. Additionally, groups offer opportunities to recognize and discuss assumptions, validate feelings, and become more observant of the layers involved in moving from reaction, to deeper perception of a situation or response. While reflective practice is recognized and used in many early childhood settings, much remains to be done before the value of reflective practice and supervision groups is fully understood and well integrated into all layers of systems and programs aimed at serving young children and families.

What does Research and Evaluation Tell Us About How Reflective Practice Groups of Various Kinds Support the Field of Infant, Young Child, and Family Services?

Research and evaluation of reflective practices such as individual and group supervision for infant, young child and family programs is uneven and emergent, spanning particular disciplines and areas of practice. Despite the limitations of the existing research, reflective practice has been found to:

- Contribute to the resilience and adaptability of staff and teams (Turner, 2009).
- Decrease the expulsion of boys of color from child development and day care settings (Albritton et al., 2019; Shivers et al., 2021).
- Increase the reflective capacities of participants (Virmani, 2010; Barron, 2019).
- Help participants understand and apply learning about early development and intervention, the impact of trauma, and other content areas specific to their work (Fitzsimmons, 2018).
- Reduce the secondary effects of traumatic stress and burnout that can occur when working with populations who have experienced trauma, high levels of inequality in accessing needed services, employment and housing (Barron, 2019; Butler, 2017; Woltman, 2008).
- Reduce staff turnover (National Center for Crime and Delinquency, 2006).
- Increase participants' ability to look at themselves and others to consider racial, cultural, and social identities, areas of privilege and power, and circumstances of real and perceived oppression. Consider both individual and collective blind spots related to racism and actions taken to be more anti-racist (Silverman, 2019).
- Increase the quality of services provided to children and families (Bernstein et al., 2013).

A compelling meta-analysis by Davidson and colleagues (2014) on the use of group work in learning settings has shown that learners:

- Increase job satisfaction and a sense of the value of one's work.
- Develop deeper understanding of material
- Learn more and retain knowledge longer
- Develop social and leadership skills

Two recent reviews provide more information about particular areas of consultation practice:

- West and colleagues (2022) describe consultation needs related to home visiting programs and review some of the existing research in the home visiting field.
- The Georgetown University Center of Excellence has published an annotated bibliography that also details outcomes of various studies of consultation to child care. (Center of Excellence for Infant and Early Childhood Mental Health Consultation, 2021).

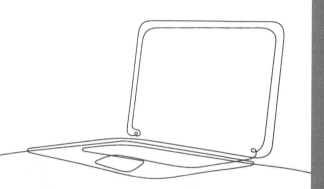

Online Resources – Section 1

 Reflective Supervision: What We Know and What We Need to Know to Support and Strengthen the Home Visiting Workforce. (ACF, DHHS)

 Secondary Traumatic Stress Core Competencies for Trauma Informed Support and Supervision: Cross Disciplinary Version.

 Using Reflective Supervision to Support Trauma-Informed Systems for Children (Multiplying Connections)

 Can Preschool Expulsion Be Prevented?

 Status of the Evidence for Infant and Early Childhood Mental Health Consultation (iecmh.org)

 Early Childhood Mental Health Consultation: Results of a Statewide Random-Controlled Evaluation.

SECTION 2
PLANNING REFLECTIVE PRACTICE GROUPS

> *"It does not do to leave a live dragon out of your calculations if you live near one"*
> **—J.R.R. Tolkien**

Considering the Purposes of a Reflective Practice Group

Reflective practice groups describe groups in varied settings that have distinctly different purposes. For simplicity we use the term reflective group facilitator for anyone who has the responsibility to hold and facilitate a group of any kind. The groups will have distinct characteristics based on the group's purposes, experience levels of the participants, and other factors related to individual characteristics and needs of participants and their programs.

Below is a list of some of the possible categories of reflective practice. There will be others that organizations and programs define.

- ◆ **Reflective practice group supervision** provides an opportunity for interventionists of all kinds such as mental health clinicians, social workers, home visitors, early interventionists, teachers, medical professionals and others involved in some form of service with children and families an opportunity to reflect together and learn from each other's insights and knowledge about their work. These groups are often provided for staff with different job categories. Supervisors, leaders, and others often have their own spaces and times for reflective group supervision. We distinguish groups as reflective practice supervision groups when the reflective group facilitator has responsibilities for the "whole job" including the practice requirements of the group participants. However, in many instances, reflective group facilitators also have individual meetings with staff to address individual needs, support documentation and review performance. These kinds of group reflective practice sessions might be called team support meetings if members from a particular unit, program, or geographical area gather. Group reflective practice supervision can be very powerful in building a sense of mission, engendering mutual support, increasing understanding of diverse perspectives, and providing a space where the group feels held and contained.

- ◆ **Reflective practice consultation groups** are ongoing and can be an important part of support system for staff who are working with parents and children in a variety of settings. These groups usually focus on the interactive aspects of the work with children and parents and the needs of the staff who support them. Consultation in child development and care settings is included in this category. However, the structure and staffing needs of childcare centers often means that consultation may be conceptualized as a 1:1 activity where a consultant observes and then meets with an individual teacher. Nevertheless, some consultation in child care settings is able to be structured so that the consultant meets regularly with a teaching team or a group of staff. Consultation with infant and early childhood development and child care groups has expanded since recent evaluation studies demonstrated their value in supporting staff to understand and improve their ability to work effectively with children and families of color. (Albritton et al., 2019).

- **Reflective practice affinity groups** provide support and consultation around a specific role or function. This could include consultation, or support of a particular function or role, e.g. groups for reflective supervisors, reflective practice facilitators, center directors, team leaders or others who have a job managing, supporting, and guiding others. These groups can be within or across agencies. Recently, affinity groups based on racial categories have also grown in popularity.

- **Communities of practice** are groups that focus on improving a specific area of shared interest or concern, building relationships through activities and learning. For example, groups of speech therapists from several agencies or communities may form a group to build their skill working with second language learners who are grappling with a speech impediment.

- **Short Term Reflective Practice Groups** may address a specific purpose or impact on the participants. For example, day care staff members who experienced an intrusion onto the site by a threatening individual, or a program who is merging with another agency, expanding or contracting with outside services because of fluctuations in funding. These types of groups usually find the shared group experience useful, particularly when the intent and processes of the group are clear.

- **Reflective Practice Focus Groups** build understanding through by discussing matters related to topics such as diversity, racial justice, equity and inclusion, traumatic events in a community or workplace, impending organizational change, service to new populations such as recent immigrants from a particular area, or other changes that impact the work done by the staff.

- **Reflective Practice Planning Groups** include leaders, administrative and planning staff working together with service providers and possibly community members and clients on program development, staff support and retention, program mission and goals, other funding, administrative, or mission related topics that drive planning efforts.

- **Reflective Practice Community** or cross agency groups of individuals doing work together on teams or in centers who want to improve their outcomes, increase staff collaboration and solidarity, and reduce stress by building more reflective capacity and mutual support.

- **Reflective Practice Training Groups** such as Child Parent Psychotherapy, FAN, Circle of Security®, or Healthy Steps meet together to discuss application of principles and interventions related to the model they are learning. Such groups could also form to discuss new service areas such as pop up playgroups, or including mental health staff in pediatric clinics.

It is crucial that group planners take the time to clearly state and communicate the intention of the group, when and how often the group is to meet, and any evaluation criteria.

Planning wisely contributes to the success of a group. The fantasy writer J.R.R Tolkien once stated, "It does not do to leave a live dragon out of your calculations, if you live near him." Although Tolkien was likely not referencing reflective practice directly, the metaphor he created is useful to elucidate considerations necessary for reflective practice groups. These "dragons" might be unduly heavy workloads that make group attendance difficult, a past group that ended poorly and caused tension among the staff, racial divides or feelings of inequity, lack of clarity about the purpose, a lack of felt safety that restrains group participation. Reviewing any past evaluations and interviewing previous and proposed participants can be useful in discovering dragons that may require recognition and taming.

Involving Participants in Planning

Since clarity about the purpose and meaning of a group is so central to its success, it can be helpful for planners to involve a variety of staff in discussing and shaping details of a group beforehand. When this joint planning, or co-construction, happens in a reflective practice group the agreed upon purpose of the group is more likely to become a kind of touchstone that is visited as needed. This clarity also helps participants assess, evaluate and work with the facilitator to make changes and adjustments as the group evolves. It is advisable to consider practical issues such as recruitment and selection of members, financial support, timing, location, and any barriers to participation such as lack of privacy, access to materials, scheduling, or workload.

Pre-Group Contact and Information Sharing with Individual Group Members
How individuals hear about a group is important because the source of the information can influence an individual's decision to participate. Providing clear written information that can be shared with participants in advance is essential. Questions or concerns can be addressed during staff meetings, phone calls, or e-mail exchanges.

Some writers and practitioners advocate strongly for individual meetings with participants before a group begins. While not always feasible, these kinds of meetings can clarify purpose, help an individual feel known, answer questions and instill a sense of safety and meaning that help build productive groups.

Planning for Openness, and a Stance of Collaboration
Transparency and self-awareness on the part of the facilitator can support group safety. It is essential that the reflective facilitator is introduced to new groups in writing and in person in ways that acknowledge their social location, identities, vulnerabilities, and passions. This information should be shared when announcing and forming the group as well as during group meetings.

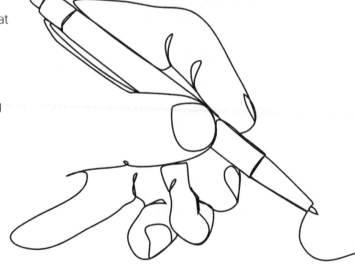

This is an example of a short written bio that could be elaborated in initial meetings.

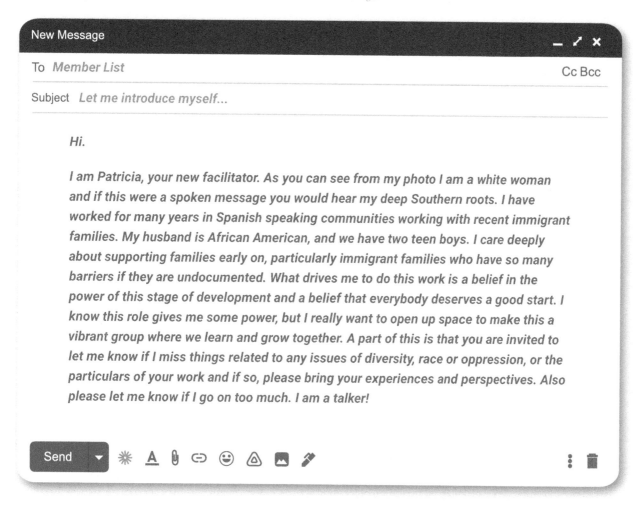

New Message — ↗ ✕

To *Member List*   Cc Bcc

Subject *Let me introduce myself...*

Hi.

I am Patricia, your new facilitator. As you can see from my photo I am a white woman and if this were a spoken message you would hear my deep Southern roots. I have worked for many years in Spanish speaking communities working with recent immigrant families. My husband is African American, and we have two teen boys. I care deeply about supporting families early on, particularly immigrant families who have so many barriers if they are undocumented. What drives me to do this work is a belief in the power of this stage of development and a belief that everybody deserves a good start. I know this role gives me some power, but I really want to open up space to make this a vibrant group where we learn and grow together. A part of this is that you are invited to let me know if I miss things related to any issues of diversity, race or oppression, or the particulars of your work and if so, please bring your experiences and perspectives. Also please let me know if I go on too much. I am a talker!

Send ▾   ✳ A ᯾ ⚲ ☺ △ ▨ ✐   ⋮ 🗑

Written Agreements

Written agreements outline the details of a reflective practice group in terms of intent, schedule, logistics, confidentiality, and expectations of the participants including attendance. The agreement should communicate what and to whom the facilitator will report in terms of attendance and the participant's responsibility to report any absences in advance.

The agreements related to participation help participants understand what will happen in the group, how both their cognitive and emotional responses to case material and situations are valued, and also how these processes are protected and shaped by a clear purpose and the leadership of the reflective practice group facilitator. These agreements can be considered prior to the beginning of the group, but the participants need ample time at the onset of the group to review the agreements, seek clarification, and discuss any changes the group may want to make to enhance the group's clarity, purpose, and safety.

See sample agreements in the resource section and more details about these kinds of agreements in Section 3. We also recommend this material as a basis for thinking about both safety and bravery in groups.

Group Size

Group size is an important consideration in the planning of any group. In one of the few studies that considers the actual size of groups, Knight (2010) studied a group from a psychology training group in the U.K. and emphasized a group with a maximum of 10 to 13 participants was optimal, and even ethically necessary, to minimize participant distress and maximize perceived value. However, other writers and organizations discuss smaller groups of 5 to 9 (Heffron et al., 2016). To most accurately determine what is the best size, it is essential to consider the purpose of the groups, length of the meetings, group facilitator skills, program resources, the experience of the participants, participant availability, and the number of times a group will meet. For example, if the purpose of a group is for participants to discuss dilemmas in their work in order to build particular skills, there must be enough time for this engagement with all members. This means that very short term groups with this purpose should have fewer members, and longer term groups could be a bit larger.

In-person Groups

In addition to the basics above, some of the considerations for planning in-person groups are:

- A private, easily accessible, and comfortable space.
- Minimize interruptions and distractions.
- Comfortable seating arranged in a circle or in a configuration where all group members can see one another. Beware the hard wooden or metal chair, or if this is all that is available, consider finding cushions or advising participants that these may be necessary.
- Tea, coffee, and snacks help people feel nurtured. If no funds are available for snacks, members can rotate bringing in snacks for the group.
- A white board or other space or screen to write or share words or visuals is helpful.
- If possible, post any shared resources or follow up communication between meetings on an online site such as Padlet or Basecamp.

CONSIDERATIONS FOR **IN-PERSON GROUP**

| A private, comfortable space | Minimize interruptions | Comfortable, circularly arranged seating | Tea, coffee, and snacks | White board or screen | On-line site to post resources shared and follow up discussions |

Online Groups

Prior to 2020 most reflective practice groups happened in person. During the COVID-19 pandemic, with varying degrees of precautions mandated or advised, many more reflective practice groups used an online platform such as Zoom™, Teams™ or Skype. Practitioners have learned that despite the lack of in-person contact, meaningful reflective work can be done online, and many groups continue to use this format because it is convenient and cost-saving. Reflective facilitators can do their work from a distance, saving travel costs for facilitators, participants, and sponsoring programs. Participants who are scattered across cities, regions or even continents, can more easily gather thus building larger support networks and exposure to multiple perspectives. Despite these advantages, hosting groups online requires more work to engage participants effectively. "Zoom Fatigue," and a sense of increased social isolation, depression and stress are real challenges associated with the use of video-conferencing and should be addressed proactively. Video-conferencing features that allow smaller group size can be considered to foster a sense of connection and togetherness.

Some elements that help online groups to function effectively include:

◆ **Maintaining a sense of active presence.** Before the group begins, consider how to approach discussions about being on or off camera, frequency of breaks, and expectations for participants who need to go off screen briefly (who are recommended to signal this to the facilitator through chat rather than just leave).

◆ **Employing brief, individual meetings online before a group begins.** This practice allows the facilitator to meet participants as well as to orient participants to the features of the online platform, discuss any technical questions or equipment needs, clarify procedures for signing on, and address general issues about participating. It will be important to explain that the platform is only open to members and how the platform is protected for confidentiality and HIPAA compliance.

◆ **Sharing written introductions.** In advance of the meeting, participants can write a paragraph about themselves using reflective prompts to share information such as their background, what they want out of the group, and hopes they have for their participation. These can be shared on a group site or platform if available.

◆ **Attend to the physiological and polyvagal challenges presented by online groups.** Group facilitators will need to consider what it takes to promote a sense of real connection. This includes having a clear, well lit screen, seeking eye contact, considering tone of voice and eye contact, and animating the upper body, arms and hands. Having group members wave together or develop other group signals is helpful (Porges, 2020).

◆ **Written agreements for online groups** should be specific to the web-based setting. Group discussions and agreements should consider how to minimize possible disruptions, such as ringing phones, incoming emails, and texting during a reflective group session.

◆ **Using activities such as movement, breath and grounding exercises** to create a sense of connection and common purpose. At the end of this section, see Online Resources – Sections II for a list of suggested activities and exercises.

◆ **Engage online groups using the interactive features of Zoom or other platforms.** Break out rooms, whiteboards, stamping, Mentimeter features such as word clouds and polls can all support interaction.

◆ **Self care.** Invite group members to bring food or beverages of their choice to add self care and a sense of sharing to the group. Short breaks and/or movement and stretch activities help with fatigue and should be built in at least every 45 minutes.

- ◆ **Maintain group process.** Many facilitators are currently working in an online environment that provides a variety of modalities for communicating during a meeting, such as group (chat) and individual (direct message) features. To support a true group process, we recommend that as people gather, the individual chat function remains open. Once the work of the group begins, we suggest that the mode for individual chatting is limited to allow members to only message facilitators directly and used if the member needs to leave the meeting for an emergency. Messages to everybody in the group can remain open and can be helpful for those wishing to raise questions or add comments. It is important to note, side chats and private messages to the facilitator can create a situation where not everyone is fully present with each other. The host can let participants know that individual messaging between participants is not available during the group meeting.

- ◆ **Encourage sharing between sessions.** Online learning platforms, forums or discussion boards, may be useful as an addition to promote discussions or resource sharing between groups. Suggested platforms include SharePoint, Google-Groups, Google Drive, Microsoft Teams, Padlet, and Miro Board.

Reflective Practice Groups that Take Place in Program Settings

Reflective practice groups in agencies and organizations are most effective when they are fully sanctioned, understood and supported by the agency and systems in which they operate. These practices include: Allocation of resources to support individuals participating in the groups to ensure the time spent participating in the groups is considered part of the work activity sanctioned by the agency. This might involve adjusting caseloads or other responsibilities so that staff get the support and reflective opportunities they need to do their work.

- ◆ Clear communication about the group(s) purpose(s) and requirements for participation to be delivered to group members. Other staff should be informed about sanctioned group activities so they avoid scheduling competing meetings or activities over the regular group time.

- ◆ Staff from the agency who facilitate reflective practice groups should receive their own reflective support or supervision for this work.

- ◆ Alignment of administrative activities with reflective practice approaches so that other organizational functions such as committees, training, team and staff meetings feature an emphasis on reflection with invitations to bring forward different views and perspectives.

- ◆ Participants should be supported to bring difficult issues that have been discussed in the group back to their individual program supervisor for review. For example, if a case is discussed in a group supervision and the participant now feels that they would like to alter an intervention approach or add a new resource, this should be discussed with the supervisor who has responsibility for the case.

- ◆ Discussion and determination of agreed upon practices outlining how a reflective facilitator will provide feedback about programmatic concerns, such as policies, supervisory or managerial issues, or resource needs to administrative staff without violating norms of group confidentiality. Best practices would include: (1) discuss this need in the group and provide encouragement and support for staff on finding a way to address issues directly with appropriate staff, (2) if it seems ethically necessary to bring an issue to the attention of program staff, group members should be informed about the communication and that the issue would be identified as a group concern, not that of a particular individual, and (3) discussions with the administrative staff beforehand would clarify group expectations stressing the need for sturdy boundaries on confidentiality for the groups, and clearly defined guidance about what information would be shared.

- ◆ Periodically, participants should be given opportunities to evaluate the purpose, process, and usefulness of the group.

- ◆ Reflective practice group facilitators or supervisors from outside an agency should be carefully chosen and provided with the orientation and support needed to understand the specifics of the participating agencies and populations served, organizations, and systems. The same essential points about confidentiality, feedback, attendance and complaints that were elaborated in the prior section apply to group facilitators from outside an agency. Issues related to confidentiality need to be carefully considered, and the communication between the group facilitator and the program leaders and administration should be carefully thought through. Confidentiality agreements and requirements should be clearly communicated to facilitators, group participants and program staff who are supporting the groups.

Groups Run by Professional and Community Groups

Participation in reflective practice groups outside of an agency can be useful in promoting professional growth and development, skill building in using particular models of service delivery, building collaborative efforts in systems and communities, and working in a community or system to address a community or system's need using collective action models.

Some examples would be:

◆ Reflective practice or mentoring groups connected to training in a particular model such as Child First, Nurse-Family Partnership (NFP), Child Parent Psychotherapy, the Facilitating Attuned Interactions (FAN), Circle of Security, or child care consultation. Professional Groups such as state Infant Mental Health associations may also sponsor reflective practice groups for particular purposes such as increasing a focus on diversity, equity and inclusion in services, or addressing service expansion needs in a community or region.

◆ Practitioners such as early interventionists or mental health providers who work as contractors or in private practice that want a sense of community and a place to discuss their work.

◆ Affinity groups that form across programs to help address new populations, resource sharing and coordination, or build particular kinds of knowledge or skill.

Planners have many issues to consider to set up an effective reflective practice group. As a group is set up, the choice of a facilitator is central and the questions below can help planners choose the right person for the particular group.

◆ What are the proposed reflective practice facilitator's skills and training? Does the proposed candidate have group experience, or if not would they be able to run a group more effectively with a co-facilitator or additional support?

◆ Where will the reflective practice facilitator get an opportunity to debrief and seek their own time for consultation and reflection?

◆ Does the proposed reflective practice facilitator have experience addressing issues of race, equity, culture and inclusion in their work? Are they able to recognize microaggressions or patterns of exclusion or bias and address these in a group setting in ways that expand understanding?

◆ Are there members of the proposed group who are bilingual and if so is there a bilingual facilitator available, or could a bilingual individual interested in learning group facilitation co-facilitate with a more experienced leader?

◆ If the reflective practice group is a supervisory group, have current supervisory relationships or any known staff conflicts been taken into consideration? If the group is more of a consultation group used to strengthen reflective capacity and address intervention work this may be less important, but these prior relationships should still be considered thoughtfully.

◆ If the agency or program is using its own staff to facilitate reflective practice groups, have accommodations been made so that those individuals have the support, training, and time they need to do the job well?

◆ If an outside facilitator is used, how will this individual be oriented to the agency and team in a way that is sensitive to issues of confidentiality? How will the facilitator learn about the agency's intentions, logistics, and culture? How can the facilitator access support?

◆ What will need to be done to fully prepare an outside facilitator to build and support a group? What might someone from an agency need to know to take on this role?

KEY QUESTIONS FOR PLANNERS OF REFLECTIVE PRACTICE GROUPS

WHAT ARE THE FACILITATOR'S SKILLS AND TRAINING?

WHERE CAN THE FACILITATOR DEBRIEF AND SEEK CONSULTATION?

CAN THE FACILITATOR ADDRESS ISSUES OF RACE, EQUITY, AND INCLUSION?

HOW WILL LANGUAGE BARRIERS BE ADDRESSED?

HAVE SUPERVISORY RELATIONSHIPS AND STAFF CONFLICTS BEEN CONSIDERED?

WHAT SUPPORTS AND ACCOMMODATIONS ARE NECESSARY?

HOW WILL THE FACILITATOR LEARN ABOUT THE AGENCY AND ACCESS SUPPORT?

WHAT ESSENTIAL INFORMATION DOES A FACILITATOR NEED?

When considering contracting with an external consultant as a group facilitator, a number of important considerations should be explored. Ideally, the facilitator:

◆ Has a combination of intervention experience and a working knowledge of the importance of reflection in early childhood settings.

◆ Has the necessary knowledge set, licensure, or certification. For example, in a FAN or Child Parent Psychotherapy consultation, the mentoring group and the reflective facilitator must be knowledgeable about the model, the underlying theories, and be able to use facilitative techniques to help participants as they begin to use the strategies of the model or approach in their work. A facilitator running a group for pre-license social workers or mental health clinicians or those seeking endorsement would need to be licensed or endorsed according to policies that allow the participants to apply those hours toward licensure/endorsement. A group for preschool teachers would require a facilitator who is familiar with the challenges and parameters of the preschool setting, understands behavioral and developmental concerns, has a capacity to hold and address relational health issues, and possesses the skills needed to help teachers consider what they bring to interactions with children and parents.

◆ Is willing to put in the work necessary to understand the program, including the specifics of the services provided, the system and organization that support the program, policies, documentation needs, and client needs.

◆ Understands the stages of group development as well as the process, structures, and approaches that encourage this development.

◆ Is able to skillfully navigate common difficulties in group encounters.

◆ Is attentive to group processes and any shifts in tone, pacing, and participation.

◆ Applies techniques that encourage reflection.

◆ Observes, listens to, contains, and responds to any complicated emotions and feelings that may arise.

◆ Has a clear sense of their own social location and is comfortable working with diverse groups. Uses their skills to help participants apply critical self-reflection and explore a deeper use of self in their work.

◆ Have an awareness of their own power and privilege and a commitment to remain aware of these concerns and discuss both in the group agreements and in the group process as these opportunities arise.

◆ Is capable of forming relationships with individuals from diverse backgrounds.

◆ Is able to perceive their own biases.

◆ Supports and encourages dialogue that promotes a deeper understanding of diversity, equity, and inclusion.

◆ Speaks the language(s) of those in the group.

Individuals from many disciplines can become reflective facilitators. It is not necessary that a reflective facilitator have exactly the same experiential background or credentials as those in the group. Reflective facilitators from a different discipline may bring knowledge or experience that enriches the overall experience of the group. However, it is essential that all reflective practice group facilitators have an awareness about the specifics of the work that the participants are doing, their disciplinary focus, and prior training they have received as well as knowledge of the organizations and systems they are working with and the nature of the populations served.

No matter what their background, reflective practice group facilitators must be able to support the growth of the participants' skills more by using reflective facilitation skills than by teaching or telling the group or inserting their own individual focus on how to do a particular job. The facilitator should be able to strategically consider when and how to bring in key pieces of information or useful theories that can support the group process. For example, the reflective facilitator might ask a question of the group or share a small piece of information and elicit discussion. Facilitators also can summarize or highlight information flowing from the group.

What Kind of Support Does a Reflective Practice Facilitator Need to Run a Group?

Reflective practice group facilitators need a safe place to talk about the progress, struggles, and successes of the group. All facilitators should have an opportunity to meet regularly with a supervisor or consultant who can help them grow their skills and navigate and group concerns. For those who are just starting out, training and reflective support are essential as they learn new skills and navigate a new role.

Having a more experienced facilitator co-facilitate with a less experienced one can help the newer facilitator build essential skills.

Evaluative processes for a reflective practice group will vary widely based on the setting and the resources available. Evaluation is always essential for the facilitator to monitor their own effectiveness and support ongoing planning. Evaluation can also be useful for program leaders because it can help them understand how participants are experiencing the groups and whether additional support or intervention is needed for the groups to be effective. How much evaluation is needed depends on the availability of resources, including time and planning.

No matter how brief or extensive the evaluation process, it is essential that it be built from the purpose, goals, and intentions of the group.

Below are some suggested evaluation strategies.

- At a minimum each time a reflective group meets, there should be at least a few minutes to pause and reflect about what they are taking away from the session,consideration of processes within the group, and consideration of anything they want to carry forward to the next group. The reflective group facilitator shapes the questions based on the stated intentions of the group. For example, if a group's intentions were stated as 1) building reflective practice skills and 2) Reducing workplace stress, the facilitator might ask the participants what they were taking away related to skills and feeling more able to handle stress.

A variation on this basic process is referred to as a Delta-Plus activity. In this process at the end of a reflective group practice meeting facilitators simply ask and later record what went well and what could be improved.

- As indicated on the ARC diagram on page 27, it is important for the group facilitator to take time to record and reflect on important takeaways, aspects of the group process, key moments in the group, and their own experiences and insights. This information becomes both a record and a planning tool. See Appendix 7: Tracking Content & Process in a Reflective Practice Group.

- The use of short confidential surveys after each session, or at least 2 points in the process is highly recommended. These evaluations can be done electronically on platforms like Survey Monkey, Microsoft forms or Qualtrics, and the results can be tracked from group to group showing growth and pointing out concerns within the group. Evaluations can be done each session and reviewed by the facilitators to pull out themes, strengths of the group, emerging skills, and concerns. See Appendix 8: Participant Evaluation Form Sample.

- At the end of a group or a series of groups, programs with access to evaluation resources may want to collect data using a focus group process bringing selected members together for in depth interviews from which evaluators distill data.

- More specialized evaluations such as looking at stress and burnout, or a specific participant capacity, or program outcome may require both pre and post measures and more careful planning using team or community members knowledgeable about evaluation. See Appendix 9: Measuring Reflective Supervision within Home Visiting.

Online Resources – Section 2

 Best Practice Guidelines for Reflective Supervision/Consultation

 Georgetown University's Center of Excellence for Early Childhood Mental Health Consultation to Infant and Early Childhood Programs.

 Reflective Group Supervision and Some Guidelines

 Center of Excellence for Infant and Early Childhood Mental Health Consultation | SAMHSA

 Demystifying Reflective Practice

 The Reflective Case Discussion Model of Group Supervision

SECTION 3

IMPLEMENTATION- GROUP STRUCTURES AND REFLECTIVE PRACTICE GROUP FACILITATOR SKILLS

"You should not underestimate the power you have to affirm the humanity and dignity of the people who are around you. And when you do that, they will teach you something about what you need to learn about human dignity, but also what you can do to be a change agent."

—Bryan Stevenson

Stages and Phases of Group Process: How a Reflective Practice Group Unfolds

While each reflective practice group possesses its distinctive composition and evolution, shaped by the group's objectives, participants' backgrounds and experiences, and the contextual dynamics of their communities and agencies, a recognizable sequence often emerges in the group's journey. Scholars like Yalom and Leszcs (2020), Tuckman (1977), and Christopher Johns (2022), among others, have delineated these phases and processes of groups across diverse settings and objectives.

- ◆ **Starting Out** – Even if a facilitator has extensive experience with reflective practice groups, and has planned thoughtfully, group members may enter with some hesitance or skepticism. The facilitator at this stage is working to instill a sense of meaning, welcome, safety, and familiarity among the members. Group members may seek to gain connection with the facilitator during this phase or may remain aloof for some time and require invitation and validation from facilitator. Always in this phase it is essential that group agreements are presented, discussed, and amended by the group. Another alternative is for the group agreements to be developed with the group rather than amending an existing set. This is the time in the group to create safety and a sense of common purpose. Although the group facilitator can begin to introduce critical self-reflection, to the group, at this stage, it is best for the facilitator to model it themself.

- ◆ **Finding a Rhythm** – Usually after several sessions a group has developed a process and group norms, and has established a rhythm of proceeding from one meeting to the next. Group norms are an essential reference point. The rhythm includes a beginning, middle and an end. In this phase, conflict, misunderstanding, disagreements, and uncomfortable moments of stony silence can emerge. As group members begin to settle into the group, the facilitator can begin to gently encourage participants to consider new perspectives as they begin to expand their self knowledge and awareness.

- ◆ **Cohesiveness and Purpose** – Group members focus on achieving common goals. The group is characterized by trust, experience and mutual support. Appreciation for the group responses and dialogue can be observed at times. Different points of view are valued as ways to learn as long as it is channeled through group norms. Tensions, or even ruptures may occur, but the group has enough strength to stay in the process to work through these challenges most of the time.

- ◆ **Wondering/Evaluating/Concluding** – At this point a group often begins to look at itself with more awareness of the group experience and consider the utility of the group either as a part of an ongoing process or as a meaningful experience. Has the group worked to meet the intended goals? Were there any surprises? What adjustments might need to be made if the group continues? Has the group become essential? If the group is concluding, what has been learned? What are group members taking away from this experience?

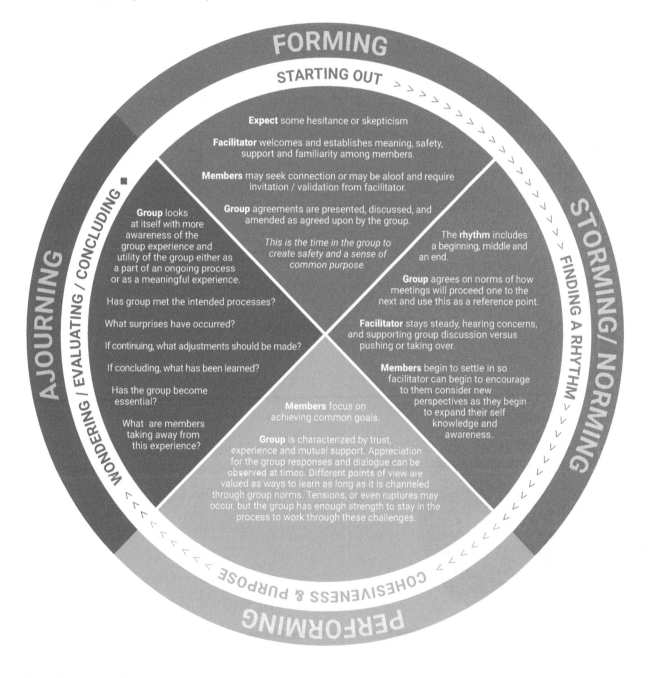

Time frames for these phases vary widely with individuals and circumstances and for a variety of reasons. Some groups take longer to move to the cohesiveness and purpose stage and some may never reach that stage.

How does a Reflective Facilitator Structure and Adjust Sessions?

Tracking and reflecting on what is happening within the group allows the facilitator to adjust their plan in order to better meet the group's needs. The facilitator should be aware of phases in the life of a group and attend to what is happening for group members in any given moment. It is also important for the facilitator to take time to reflect about the meaning of the group's behavior before and after sessions.

For example, a facilitator might observe whether the group process flows easily or seems constrained, notice who contributes a lot and who doesn't, or sense the group's comfort level when it comes to addressing matters of race or class. It may be helpful for the facilitator to monitor these processes over time and to have an opportunity to discuss this in supervision or consultation with another. See Appendix 7: Group Tracking Form, Appendix 4: Sample Reflection Questions, and Appendix 6: Skill Assessment for Reflective Group Facilitators.

The ARC of Engagement from the FAN model offers a useful sequence to approach structuring a group meeting. First, and most importantly, is taking the time to relax and center oneself before engaging with the group. This might include reviewing past notes or planned activities for the session. After the session, facilitators should take at least 10 minutes to settle and write some notes regarding their observations of group processes, emergent themes, concerns, or breakthroughs.

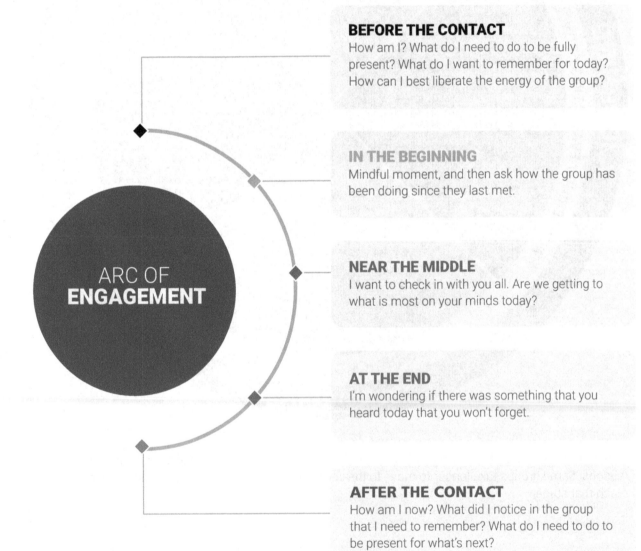

ARC OF ENGAGEMENT

BEFORE THE CONTACT
How am I? What do I need to do to be fully present? What do I want to remember for today? How can I best liberate the energy of the group?

IN THE BEGINNING
Mindful moment, and then ask how the group has been doing since they last met.

NEAR THE MIDDLE
I want to check in with you all. Are we getting to what is most on your minds today?

AT THE END
I'm wondering if there was something that you heard today that you won't forget.

AFTER THE CONTACT
How am I now? What did I notice in the group that I need to remember? What do I need to do to be present for what's next?

Concept used by permission from Linda Gilkerson, Erikson Institute, Chicago, Illinois

Focusing on the Unique Nature of Each Group

After a group has been planned and formed, the facilitator's focus shifts to engaging with and meeting the needs of group members. Things to consider at this stage include:

◆ How familiar are members with group models of reflective practice and with one another?

◆ Is the group already familiar with the facilitator? If not, the group may need more time for questions, connecting, and building trust.

◆ Is the purpose of the group known and valued? Is it a new kind of voluntary or required group that may need further discussion or clarification?

◆ How can the reflective practice group facilitator demonstrate that the participants really have a voice in shaping ongoing content?

◆ If there are known conflicts or tensions among group members, it is important to address this before the group meets. If this is not possible, the facilitator should receive additional support to address these issues.

Individualizing Schedules and Rituals for Each Group

Groups develop their own personality, but structure, rituals and thoughtful ongoing planning support the unleashing of the power and creativity of the group. Armed with answers to at least some of the questions listed above gathered from planners of the group and if possible individual meetings with participants, the facilitator can construct a simple agenda and consider processes and rituals that set the stage for the group.

This starts with a rough draft of a schedule that should include an opening and connecting activity, the main content, and, finally, an opportunity to reflect on and integrate that content. A ritual is created through repetition. Rituals might include: how the room is arranged or prepared, the presence of refreshments, or a familiar greeting. Some groups may have a ritual object that they use to designate who speaks first. Rituals can also be incorporated into any part of the group process using a consistent prompt to signal a shift into a new phase or activity. For example, using the prompt, "Let's take a breath together before we begin" can be used before starting each session or before starting a new activity within a session. Midway through each session, a facilitator might ask, "Are we getting to what you most wanted to explore today?" Or, at the end of each session ask, "What do you most want to hold onto from our time together today?"

Reflection and Mindfulness as Preparation for the Reflective Practice Group

The ARC of Engagement on page 27 is from the FAN model and is used to highlight how important it is for the facilitator to come to a state of relaxed readiness before each group and also to take time after the session to reflect on the what happened and what needs to be tracked and remembered for the next time the group meets.

Before Each Meeting Begins

Mindful self regulation involves taking some time to come to a calm and prepared state, using breathing or other mindfulness approaches as needed, reviewing any notes from prior sessions, and any activities or prompts that will ground and center the group in the present. These links are in the Online Resources – Section 3 at the end of this section as well as in the Resources section at the end of this guide.

Grounding or Mindful Self Regulation Activities for Session Participants

Grounding or mindfulness exercises can help group participants transition from a busy activity to a calm and attentive state. A simple grounding/mindfulness activity is to sit with a tall spine, take a few deep breaths, and consciously ask participants to silently draw attention to what they see, hear, and can touch. Sometimes activities can be used to energize the group. These activities are in the Online Resources – Section 3 at the end of this section as well as in the Resources section at the end of this guide.

As a facilitator gets to know a group, it is important to offer the possibility for the participants to contribute to the connecting, grounding and mindfulness activities using quotes, movement, their own spiritual practices, stories, poetry, music, or images.

Connecting Activity for Session Participants

After a few minutes of greeting and orientation, groups often start with a simple connecting activity to build a sense of community. For a first meeting rather than going around reciting resumes out loud, it can be more engaging to have an activity that shares some personal meaning. An example of an activity that is particularly suited to a first meeting might be having participants give a 1-2 sentence story about their first name. E.g. "At school and work I was always Mary, but with my dad's family I am Madianka, Czech for little Mary." Other options are to share a family tradition or ritual that has a positive meaning for the participant, or something about them that others would not be likely to know. See Appendix 7: Suggestions for Connecting Activities.

The purpose of these activities is getting to know one another, or as the group, to reconnect and deepen relationships. Activities can also be used to link with emergent themes in the group. As the group evolves, the connecting activities may not be needed, or alternatively, participants can be assigned the job of bringing in an activity.

Investing Deeply in Group Safety and Bravery

Reflective practice groups have the potential to be a trustworthy space where complex feelings, thoughts, confusing experiences, and broader perspectives can be held, explored and contained. These spaces are enriched when participants expand these explorations with increasing awareness of their own identities, those of others, and the forces that shape the work we do and the clients we serve. For most groups this takes time as participants can come with generation wounds, scars of trauma, or cautions from prior groups where they may have felt marginalized. As we have noted in the Section 2, participants should always be given a suggested list of guidelines for group process for review and discussion. These can be personalized and amended as needed. Sample guidelines inspired by the work of Hardy and Bobes (2015) listed in Appendix 3 address notions related to power, privilege, race and social location as well as more general considerations for group interaction that are important to discuss as the group begins. Providing the group time to discuss, fully understand, add or subtract, and tailor the language in these guidelines to their own circumstances and language is essential. This process can be time consuming and is a needed up front cost that creates a sense of investment in the group and increases the likelihood that participants will risk discussing in a vulnerable and open manner. The guidelines can be referred back to as necessary and new guidelines can be added as needed.

Starting "The Work" in Groups

When the broad purpose of a group is clear, and basic understanding of agreed upon guidelines is established, the ongoing work of the group can proceed. E.g. If discussing difficult cases and building intervention skills is the purpose, participants can rotate presenting a particular aspect of a case or participants can be asked to bring in a particular dilemma that is troubling them, or alternatively something they felt went well. There are various ways that case material can be discussed, and facilitators should take the time to discuss this with the group and even change the process if needed after a few sessions. If addressing how to expand or improve services is the purpose, this focus can be started by brainstorming desired outcomes, listening to stories, reviewing and discussing data and then working with participants to consider obstacles or pathways that will move towards a desired goal. Involving the group in figuring out the specifics of how to get into the work or create the specific agenda sets a standard for collaboration. For example, should only one case be presented or will shorter examples suit the needs of the group. Sample vignettes can be used if participants are initially uncomfortable sharing their own experiences. In a planning or learning group, these same principles will apply. Near the midpoint of the meeting time, the reflective facilitator can use the FAN question, "are we getting at what you most wanted to talk about in this situation?" This question often opens up a deeper layer of discussion and collaboration among the group.

Ending Process for Each Session
The ending process should be a reflective integration of what has happened in the group and how it relates to the participants' work. It should start with a brief summary by the facilitator which also highlights aspects of the group's process. For example, " I really admire the way that as a group you supported each other to discuss both of these cases which involve so much sadness, loss and uncertainty. Jen's discomfort with the family's decision really helped some of us think about how our own prior experiences can come up when big issues are at stake"

In addition to discussion, there are many creative ways to gather this information using mentimeter tools, chat, white boards or individual slips of paper that get written, exchanged, and read by another person if the group is in-person. Sometimes facilitators also add a short grounding or mindfulness activity at the end of a session.

ENDING THE SESSION **SUMMARY PROMPTS**

? What is one thing you want to hold onto from today's work?

? What are you noticing about yourself and your work that you want to hold onto or continue to consider next time?

? What did you hear from a colleague, feel or think about today that you won't forget?

? Is there anything from today that you want to carry forward in your work with families?

? Are there any things we discussed today that you feel grateful for?

? Is there something from this meeting that is unsettled or will need additional follow up?

After the Reflective Practice Group Ends

Again referencing the FAN ARC of Engagement, it is recommended that the period after the end of the group include some time for the reflective facilitator to settle, untangle the themes and events of the group, and document what happened and how this will impact or potentially carry over to the next session. This tracking of the group process allows for reflection on the events of the group in order to use this information to support the continued development of robust and meaningful reflective dialog at the next meeting. These links are in the Online Resources – Section 3 at the end of this section as well as in the Resources section at the end of this guide.

Creating Continuity: Using Material from Prior Sessions to Plan and Begin Next Sessions

Here are some samples of focused prompts or provocations that can be used to create continuity from one group to another.

Thanks to Jose's initial question last week about why dads never come to the parent meetings that hit home with so many of you, we are going to work together today to think about ways that we can as a group figure out how to involve fathers and partners more actively.

Last week we were able to think about ending with a family in ways that help them see how they have grown and several of you remarked that this discussion helped you with your good-byes. Is there anything like that needed from today's meeting?"

In our last session, we talked extensively about the problem of staff retention, and we identified several possible issues that make it hard to stay with our organization. How would it be to look at those three elements in more detail? x

Last time when we met we really grappled with how to address issues related to how to work with caregivers who really disagree about how situations should be handled. I am wondering if any of you had further thoughts about this great discussion, or were able to apply some of the great ideas that were shared last time?

Last time we thought a great deal about how we can engage families earlier, and I am wondering if anyone had any additional thoughts about that since our last meeting?

Stances, Techniques and Skills For Reflective Group Facilitators

"Individually, we are one drop. Together, we are an ocean."
—Ryunosuke Sator

Reflective Group Facilitator as an Advocate for Diversity, Equity, Inclusion and an Anti-Racist Stance

Extending Awareness of Power and Privilege and the Integration of Race, Culture, Diversity, Equity and Inclusion into Reflective Practice Groups

The discussion of what is "right or wrong" or when and how to explore the topics of race, culture, diversity, and equity in reflective practice settings can be daunting. However, in order to approach these discussions in a meaningful and expansive way, it is essential for the reflective practice group facilitator to slow down and open space for each individuals' narrative and bring an atmosphere of safety, respect, and connection into the group. In order to bring these needed dimensions, a reflective practice group facilitator needs to have taken time themselves for critical self- reflection about their own social location, beliefs, biases, privilege, comfort level, and skills. This is an ongoing and dynamic process and should be considered a lifelong pursuit.

Discussions about various facets of diversity, equity, inclusion and racial justice can trigger emotional and defensive reactions. Members can become silent, reactive, judgmental, defensive, hostile, tearful, dismissive or just check out. Additionally for the reflective practice group facilitator, fear of making the wrong statement, missing a comment that should be addressed, alienating the participants, violating trust, or causing harm in the context of an allegedly supportive relationship can become barriers that lead to avoidance of topics or situations that broadly stated are about difference.

It is understandable that facilitators might feel trepidation about pushing too hard or conversely avoiding difficult conversations. However, reflective practice group facilitators who have had ample and ongoing opportunities to think about their own identities as well as how to facilitate conversations that support others to explore these differences are more likely to be able to hold a space where these explorations feel safe enough. Creating this safety can be even more complex in a group reflective practice setting and there must be a sense of trust within the reflective practice group that allows this to begin. Harrell (2014) offers 3 steps for the explorations of these topics. These include the elicitation and disclosure of the narratives related to race, diversity and inclusion within the group and an invitation to participants to bring in these concerns, raise questions, and track their own feelings, deconstruction and unpacking the meanings and emotions as these narratives appear and provide attention and support to both the connections and the differences within the group.

This framing is helpful, but provides no easy answers. Everyone's social location narrative (gender, race, class, ethnicity, sexual orientation, religion) and their standing in the community with its triggers and memories of associated discomfort or not, is highly individualized and unique to that individual's experience of their memories. We can listen and respond with empathy and caring all the while understanding the potential impact on the individual as well as the children and families they are serving. The most important groundwork that can be laid is trust and confidence that the reflective group facilitator will notice subtle and more overt ruptures, stereotypes and biases and will be able to engage in dialogue to continue exploring and learning from the perspective of self and other.

One way to make these ideas come alive is not to respond to questions and dilemmas posed by the group with an authoritative approach, but rather to frame dilemmas, note discomfort, and prompt the group to think about this from a variety of perspectives including considering something from the perspective of a person who has potentially experienced oppression or somebody who might be frozen because they don't know how to respond. In this process the reflective facilitator keeps the dialogue moving and resists the pull to give a definitive "right" answer or move towards fixing or soothing. This said, the reflective group facilitator has the role of interrupting and making visible microaggressions which will be discussed in more detail in the following section.

"Connecting deeply and directly to what is actually happening without becoming it."
— Sharon Salzburg

Techniques and Skills For the Reflective Practice Group Facilitator

TECHNIQUE & SKILLS	EXAMPLE QUOTES
Slowing down, adding comments that pull for a slower pace	"I'd love to hear more about that." "Let's take a pause here and really mull this over."
Calling in new perspectives or ideas about a topic	"Are there other ways of understanding this situation that we haven't touched on yet?" "I hear you say stubbornness, but is there anything else that might prompt this refusal?"
De-centering authority and expertise of self as a group leader	"I suspect that some of you may have particular knowledge about this kind of situation and I wonder what you have learned from your experiences that can inform this discussion."
Questioning social location and intersectionality	"How might our own identity or beliefs impact how we hear this story?" "Do you think Ahmad might have hesitations about discussing this with someone outside of his circle."
Noting bias and assumptions in the contributions of group members	"I'm noticing that when we bring up situations with parents, we often leave out the dad's and partners. I wonder what this means in our services?" "I am hearing that Tina often dismisses her grandmother that she also depends on. Do you see any exceptions to this pattern?"
Highlighting ruptures and demonstrating an ability to hold	"Brad, your response to Carina's anger at her client's partner seemed to stir you up big time"
Noticing and responding to microaggressions, stereotypes, and expressions of bias	"Whoa. Let's stop here. I want to explore what you just said, I see it differently, and would like to know more about your take on this, Others can weigh in too." "I hear your worry, but somehow this statement does not match other values I have heard you express."
Staying with a difficult topic	"I know that thinking about this brings up lots of feelings, but I wonder if we can stay with it a bit more so that we can get more of a sense of what happened to this little guy."
Making space for those who are not participating, or topics which are avoided	"I appreciate the passion that this question brings up, but I want to pause and make space for anyone else who wants to comment or even bring in another aspect of this." "As we listen, are there any parts we are leaving out?"
Observing and commenting on patterns, processes, or omissions	"I am seeing that we have a lot to say about the father in this case, but practically nothing about the mother or her reactions to the situation. I wonder why that is and if they are hard to bring in for any reason?"
Noticing and wondering about the group's process	"I am noticing that Zia's description of her struggle to work with someone whose values conflict with hers seems to have us all thinking about our own experiences with this."
Noticing participation or lack of it	"This topic of drug use in the neighborhood at the center seems to be something that has really worried all of you. I'm wondering what it is like to discuss it together?"
Noticing qualities of the group interaction	"We are getting into some new territory, but also noting that there are just two of you in this discussion. Is there anyone else who wants to add to this idea."
Ensure that group members have an equitable opportunity to participate and direct the conversation if needed	"Carl, I think for the moment you have given us a clear picture and we are really getting your exasperation with this parent and your care for the child, and I am wondering if we could hear from others who are listening to hear their ideas about why this mom might be so afraid to let Juanito explore more at the playground."

Containing and validating	*"I feel and appreciate the weight of the complexity, sadness and uncertainty that this situation with Jaime's case brings up for us."*
Opening space for different perspectives	*"How might we see this differently if we looked at it from the point of view of the child's preschool teacher?"* *"Do these transitions seem as difficult when his uncle picks him up?"* *"What might be some possible worries this situation might bring up for that staff person?"*
Judicious self-disclosure	*"I have also experienced that deep agony of feeling pulled between two parents who love a child but can't stand each other and I suspect others have too so I am going to invite us all to listen to the details of this situation."*
Using negative capability while listening to a problem that is being brought forward	While listening to a participant, a reflective facilitator feels a strong urge to suggest a solution to the dilemma being presented because of his experience with the child's disability, but he consciously holds back despite radio silence from the group and instead comments on the situation. *"This is the kind of situation with a family that can raise so many questions. I'd love to hear more from the others in the group."*
Using and promoting critical self reflection related to social location and identity	During a reflective practice group, all group members are quick to fix a dilemma presented by a member. The reflective practice group facilitator interjects while calling for use of negative capability. *"I just want to notice that we have all rushed to a solution together, and wonder if we could hold back a bit, and think about a question or two we would want to consider before moving to a "fix"."*
Summarizing and opening space to extend	*"Let's each take a minute here to think about the messages, feelings or meanings we may be holding related to incarceration before we go ahead with our discussion of Helen's case."*
Appreciating and validating group members' contributions	*"I want to make sure I heard this right, let me know if there is anything I missed or anything anyone wants to add or question."*
Microaffirmations: Short versions of appreciation and validation can be expressed through noticing and repeating back,expressions, short comments, physical gestures	*"I so value the way that you have listened so carefully to this painful story about the little boy's medical condition, and Sonya's support of this family throughout the ordeal."* *"Wow, quite a shift"* *"You were able to spot this so clearly and help this parent express her discomfort about being able to fully understand the directions related to registering her child."*
Not knowing, avoiding premature foreclosure	*"I know you really want to know what to do but that situation has a lot of dimensions and I wonder if we could take some time to think together about this."*
Using questions to invite curiosity (See appendix for more lists of reflective questions)	*"How do the rest of you see this?"* *"What other motivation might this child have?"* *"What do you imagine the parent is most concerned about in this moment?" (See appendix for more lists of reflective questions)*
Using expertise sparingly, trying the "drop of knowledge" and explore approach	*"The way I hear this, I am wondering about possible confusion about the team leader's role. What do you make of what he is saying about his job?"*
Marking structure and choice points and time limits	*"We have a few minutes before we wrap up this topic related to everybody's self care."*
Linking parts of the session together, holding the whole, and moving towards coherence	*"Let's check back with the question Carla raised right at the beginning. Let's look at how this dilemma has been explored and what ideas have emerged?"*

The following vignette illustrates some of the complexities of addressing various issues related to diversity:

Example 3.2 Vignette

Angie is a reflective facilitator for a team of providers from a program that works with teen parents in an alternative high school.

Hada, is a Latina group member, a parent advocate providing home visits and linkage services for teen mothers and their infants. She reports being upset because one of her clients has a new boyfriend, a white man, and she worries that he will undo all the progress her client has made. On the home visit he referred to Hada as "my girl's girl". She was concerned about his multiple tattoos and wondered if any of them were gang related.

One of the other members, Terri, replies quickly saying somewhat sarcastically, what do you have against tattoos or white guys for that matter? Hada seems very uncomfortable and does not reply.

After about 30 seconds of silence and discomfort in the group, Angie comments, "Something just happened here and I feel the discomfort. Hada has some worries and the comment just now seems to have stopped us in our tracks. I wonder if anyone has any thoughts that might help us get unstuck and look at some different perspectives."

Another group member Bert, asks, "Before we talk about how we feel about tattoos, I wonder if we could hear if there are specific things that Hada is worried about that the new boyfriend will do that might hurt her client."

Hada replies, "Well, personally I have nothing against white guys, but I don't like tattoos, but what's worse is that since he has been around she has missed a bunch of her classes. I just got a call from her counselor."

Terri then responds, "Hada I did have a thought that you were against him because he is a white guy, and your client is Latina like you, and I was a little sarcastic and quick to judge, I was being a jerk... I can see that this is tough and you are worried about your client and little Jorge and that it is a heck of a lot bigger than not liking tattoos."

"We will all have to repent in this generation not merely for the hateful actions of the bad people, but for the appalling silence of the good people."
— Martin Luther King Jr.

Addressing Microaggressions in a Group

King's comment is meaningful for those who facilitate reflective practice groups or supervise others as it is a call not to be silent or avoidant when a microaggression shows up. A microaggression is defined as a statement, action or incident that is an instance of indirect, subtle intentional or unintentional discrimination against members of a marginalized group. These often seemingly innocent or uninformed remarks and actions can be hurtful to individuals, perpetuate stereotypes, and tend to shut down more meaningful conversation in a group. If they are not acknowledged or responded to in ways that expand rather than contract conversation, the group may become less safe, and exploration and authenticity may retract. Another worry about not addressing these kinds of remarks is that heightened emotions may lead to angry exchanges rather than tolerable challenges or meaningful explorations.

Reflective facilitators need to be aware of the variety and the kinds of comments that can be damaging and learn to listen for both overt and the more subtle microaggressions that are often racial in nature. Microaggressions can also be related to other biases or stereotypes about any group or identities such as gender, parenting, sexual orientation, or religion. Reflective facilitators need techniques to keep themselves grounded before speaking as well as a techniques that can interrupt and make a microaggression more visible when it occurs and rocks a group. Facilitators also need to recognize their own sensitivities to areas where they or their families or communities have experienced harm from oppression, biases, stereotypes, or discrimination.

Here are some examples of microaggressions

EXAMPLES OF **MICROAGRESSIONS** AND *RESPONSES*

MICOROAGRESSION	MICOROAGRESSION	MICOROAGRESSION	MICOROAGRESSION	MICOROAGRESSION
"I don't see color."	"These people just don't care as much about education as we do."	"Men really are not so good at this kid stuff and should not be parenting on their own."	"I have a hard time trusting somebody who isn't Christian."	"This neighborhood used to be nice before all those immigrants moved in."
"I am wondering if anyone in the group sees this in a different way?"	*"Let's take a minute and think about this."*	*"This statement seems to exclude a lot of the folks that we are working with."*	*"I wonder if we can make such a broad statement, does anyone know any exceptions?"*	*"That comment really hit me in a vulnerable place, let's take a minute to think together about this."*

Microaggressions can also occur in action. For example, ignoring a comment made by an individual from a historically marginalized group or repeating something they have said earlier and attributing credit to someone else.

There is no one right way to respond as each situation is a bit different, but the first principle is always to notice and to interrupt, which makes the situation more visible and opens up the possibility for change. This might be with a question such as "Let's take a minute and think about this." "I am wondering if anyone in the group sees this in a different way?" "This statement seems to exclude a lot of the folks that we are working with" "I wonder if we can make such a broad statement, does anyone know any exceptions to this?" "That comment really hit me in a vulnerable place, let's take a minute to think together about this."

Sometimes a microaggression stirs up strong feelings with another group member, and the facilitator may have to step in to notice the rupture and the angry words and feelings in the room. Sometimes pointing out the difference between impact and intent can be helpful and open the way to a discussion that can be reparative.

Addressing microaggressions (sometimes referred to as micoraffirmations) requires some courage and practice and a strong intention to build safe space and the capacity to discuss complexity without marginalizing anyone. It is a skill set that all facilitators should aspire to acquire as it will promote growth in group participants and in turn help them learn ways that they can address these forms of communication in their work and community life. A few additional skills are listed in the skills chart in Appendix 5 and readers are also encouraged to read the work of Derald Sue (2019) and others as they build their repertoire of responses.

"Slowly, I have come to see that asking, listening, and accepting are a profound form of doing"
— Vicent Felitte M.D.

The Art and Skill of Using Reflective Questions Intentionally

Well-crafted reflective questions are a distinctive trait of skilled reflective practice group facilitators. Questions are a tool that can engage participants by prompting reflection, alternative points of view, critical self-reflection and needs for more observation or information. Questions can also breathe new life into a discussion that has gone flat or circular. A group facilitator's question can often open pathways for new thoughts to be exchanged and for a kind of a liberation of ideas that allow new perspectives to inform an idea. Group facilitators can also prompt participants to turn any judgements or strong feelings into questions so that the participants begin to take in this skill and use it in their interactions with clients and colleagues.

Here are just a few of the purposes of questions with some sample questions listed in italics.

To expand or broaden a perspective about a situation or case a member has brought.

- *How do the rest of you see this?*
- *What feelings might this behavior be hiding?*
- *What do you imagine could shift if we gained the trust of this organization?*

To hone in on an aspect of a discussion which has been left out.

- *These are such powerful observations about Joey's behavior, but I wonder what information we have about how his parents are responding to your concerns about this situation?*

To invite the speaker or participants to step outside their own values and experience to investigate the experience and world view of someone who holds a different set of identities or values.

- *What might be some reasons these parents are terrified to leave their child in the care of others?*
- *What might be making it hard for this family to ask for what they need at this point?*

To get a sense of a participant's internal resources or those of someone who is being discussed.

- *Is there anything that is helping any of you make meaning out of this tough situation?*
- *What have you learned about this family's sources of strength?*

To understand an individual's response in a group more fully.

- *Is there anything in particular about this situation that has been compelling or worrisome to you that you would be willing to share with the group?*

To encourage group members to question their own conclusions and go deeper.

- *I hear this solution, but are there any aspects of this that we may have missed or minimized?*

To learn from successes or failures.

- *What do you think helped this child make such a dramatic recovery from that incident?*
- *What's your take on why we had so few applicants for that new position?*
- *If we do this again, what do you think we could do to bring more families out for the event?*

To more deeply consider the needs or responses of others.

- *When you think about this from the perspective of a new staff member, are there any ways that this offer of additional support could seem a bit worrisome?*

To help participants analyze a success or a problematic outcome.

- *What all went into making this situation shift the way it did for that family?*
- *Is there anything any of you would consider changing if we could redo this?*

To direct attention to a proactive or future possibility.

- *This is such a convergence of negative elements for this program.*
- *What do you imagine we could do to kind of reset that would engage the community?*

To mark a shift in tone or process.

- *Something just shifted in the tone and focus in our conversation. I am wondering if there is something else one of you wants to bring forward?*

To move to a summary or a big picture look at a situation.

- *We have talked a lot about what we are doing to be more aware of bias in our programs, I am wondering what you want to hold onto from this discussion that might be of particular use in your setting?*

With any topic there is usually more than one question and over time reflective practice group facilitators develop the capacity to layer questions in ways that promote sticking with a topic for a while both to broaden and deepen understanding. Layering means building additional questions by careful attunement to what is said and what is omitted as participants speak.

Here is an example of a reflective practice supervisor/team leader talking to a group of child development specialists:

Example 3.3 Reflective Questioning

> **Participant 1**
> I just don't get why the parents aren't signing up for the second session of playgroups. It's free. I would have been there in a minute when I was a young mom.
>
> **Facilitator/team leader**
> Have any of you had a chance to ask parents about why they are not signing up?
>
> **Participant 2**
> No, I don't want to nag as they have gotten two or three messages about it.
>
> **Facilitator/team leader**
> What do the rest of you think? If you were the parent of a child might an invitation by your child's teacher be different than a text or email message?
>
> **Participant 3**
> "Asking can be risky. I think I worry deep down about rejection."
>
> **Participant 1**
> "We're being kind of timid about something we believe in. I'd be ok to ask, and I'm not so sure about those emails and messages even reaching these busy parents."
>
> **Participant 3**
> "Maybe those of us who are more comfortable could be the ones to contact the parents just to make sure they got the information.
>
> **Participant 1**
> "I also wondered what you all thought about asking those parents who have already signed up to help us?"
>
> **Facilitator / team leader**
> "These are some good ideas: Let's summarize and work out what is doable in the next few weeks before the group is set to start up again."

For more examples of reflective questions, see Appendix 4.

Reflective Facilitator as a Skilled Listener

Skilled listening is a foundational skill for reflective group facilitators. It can be complicated to hear many voices, needs, and ways of expressing feelings, all while thinking about how to deepen a discussion or even address a subtle microaggression. Here are some different ways of listening to help us build the concept of what we mean by "listening".

Planning a Response While Listening

In this style of listening, attention is on how the words or message the other person is saying impact us and the judgements we make. When we listen at this level it is primarily about gathering information so we can respond in a way that gets our point of view across or demonstrates our own knowledge or point of view on a topic. Because we are listening in this way, it is harder to let in the feelings and perspectives of the person who is talking because we are listening for the narrative content. We tend to miss a lot because we are busy formulating our own point of view for a quick response.

Attentive Listening

When we listen more carefully rather than planning a response, there is more attention on the individual or individuals who are speaking. We notice the content of what is said, the tone, pace, feelings and delivery. We are also noticing what is left out or minimized, who is speaking in the group, and what are the responses or reactions of others. We respond to what we actually hear.

Deeply Attuned Listening

Attuned listening is paying more attention to what's happening in the interactions between an individual or group you're speaking with. It means paying attention to both the content of what is being said as well as the deeper layers of meaning as well as the process of the interaction. It involves observing the ups and downs of the connections between you and the group members, and even the tension in the conversation. What is the feeling of the conversation, is it bland and cliched or is it lively and engaged? Are there risks being taken or is the conversation guarded with carefully chosen words? What are the primary thoughts and emotions in the space between the group members, and the speaker and the facilitator? What's in the space between us that's not being said? Are there topics that are avoided or minimized? What is the flow of the conversation? Who spoke first and who spoke next? How did the content of the conversation change over the course of the session? As we listen in this manner we can often use what we are picking up to formulate the next comments or questions that can deepen a conversation. Here is an example:

Angela, a participant in Hector's reflective practice group for supervisors, is discussing the difficulty she is having supervising a staff person who never shows up to supervision with anything to say. She has not mentioned the individual's ethnicity or social location and as she speaks she is visibly uncomfortable. After she describes the dilemma, the group begins asking questions including details about the differences in social location such as race, ethnicity, age, gender and sexual orientation.

The facilitator notes Angela's discomfort, and the fact that these could be relevant questions, and asks her and the participants how they want to continue? The participants ask if she can describe an interaction.

Angela agrees and Hector, notes that this would be useful, but wonders if in doing this, it would be helpful to get a fuller sense of the participant's supervisee so we can get a better sense of the difficulties.

Angela blurts out, "He's a guy and I know that men in this field are as rare as hen's teeth, so I want to like and support him, but I just feel a little talked down to when he answers me."

Hector responds by saying, "That is a meaningful detail that helps explain this dilemma, I am so glad you shared this."

Attuned and careful listening gives a message of interest, safety, and encourages exploring. The basics of responding after we have listened encourage moving more deeply and meaningfully involving all members, not just the person who has been talking.

Awareness of Transference and Countertransference Inform the Reflective Practice Group Facilitator's Stance

Transference and countertransference are important constructs from the field of psychology that are worthy of exploration no matter what your disciplinary background. Transference describes feelings that another person in a relationship or group may have about us as group leaders or individuals that is based on that individual's own earlier experiences, not the actual evolving relationship. Countertransference feelings and actions are those reactions that are rooted in the reflective group facilitator's prior experiences and can be projected onto group members. The facilitator's use of critical self-reflection, self awareness, and supported exploration of one's work over time builds awareness of these concepts and an ability to examine and consider how prior relational experience influences the present.

While these individual notions of transference and countertransference can be useful to a group facilitator particularly as they examine their own responses to a group, transference and countertransference also impacts the relationships among the group members and the families they are serving. While it is not necessary or advisable in most cases to use these terms, group facilitator's can open space to help participants consider how their prior relational experiences impact their group experiences and their work with others and how their clients' prior experiences can impact the way their clients engage with them. A related term that is often used in the infant mental health world is parallel process.

Transference

It is easy to think about how a Reflective Practice group facilitator's position may evoke earlier relationships with teachers, parents, or others who hold some authority, or even histories of domination or bullying. Given the nature of the relationship with the facilitator, a common transference involves what has been learned through familial or cultural traditions about relationships with those that hold power and authority. The memories of these earlier associations may be very clear, e.g. "He reminds me of Mr. Gregory, the leader of my youth group", or at a more subconscious level less specific of awareness, "There is something about this group leader that makes me uncomfortable."

Reflective practice group facilitators can demonstrate a degree of vulnerability by communicating the message that we are in a place where we have new opportunities to learn how to connect, try out ideas of vulnerability and transparency to see what this fresh new experience can bring. The language used by a reflective group facilitator that invites this vulnerability and transparency could sound something like this.

Example 3.5 Acknowledging transference

> *"Lynn, I am noticing and feeling that you are working very hard to get your point across, almost like you feel you won't be heard. Might this be a kind of hangover from another setting like this, or is there something we can do to let you know we are hearing your story?"*

Countertransference

The reflective group facilitator is often impacted by the feelings engendered by a group member or members. These feelings are referred to as counter-transference and when examined and brought into awareness are a terrific tool for more authentic interaction and attunement to a situation. When these feelings are out of awareness over time they can be troublesome to the well-being of the group as they can lead to judgment, distancing or playing favorites that can tip the balance in a group in unhealthy ways. Taking time to consider the responses to group members, personal insecurities when in groups, past experiences or worries about personal characteristics such as age, race, or identity can also help us to respond to particular members or the whole group in ways that are more genuine rather than too guarded, too informal, or uncomfortable. In the statements below we can hear and imagine some of the struggles with countertransference that a reflective group facilitator might be experiencing and managing.

Example 3.6 Acknowledging countertransference

> *"I was a little nervous this morning thinking about meeting all of you for the first time. It brought up some of my early fears about walking into a new class when I was in Jr. High. Will these new people like me? But beyond that, the question on the table is how do we all get to know each other rather than relive Junior high or our last group experience."*

Silence is Motivating

Giving individuals and the group time to ponder and reflect about a question is an important aspect of listening. The facilitator needs to be able to tolerate and sometimes invite silence, framing it as an opportunity for reflection and gathering ideas that can lead to more thoughtful responses. Silence in a group can be intimidating and can cause a facilitator to respond from a place of anxiety, worry that the silence will go on forever, or self doubt. Reflective facilitators can choose to use a mindfulness or grounding approach such as taking a very slow breath that helps them wait just a little bit longer before speaking into the silence.

Holding the Course and the Process-Describing and Checking

Reflective practice group facilitators need to be very conscious of their power and privilege in a group. One way to do this is not to respond to all questions and dilemmas posed by the group, but rather to describe or frame the dilemma and solicit the group to think about this from a variety of points of view. In this process the reflective facilitator keeps the dialog moving and demonstrates the value of a group more fully understanding the concerns being voiced before moving towards a solution or interpretation. These vignettes illustrate this principle.

Example 3.7 Vignettes: Describing and Checking

Vignette 1:

Alicia is a group facilitator for a group of experienced home visitors. One of them, Trini, is working with a domestic violence case and is agitated because she feels that the toddler in the family is continuing to witness violence between the parents. In the team reflective support group. Trini asks Alicia directly, "What should I do? I want to just scream at the parents to cut this out, but then I am not so sure if the parents have changed their behavior, or if the little girl is still reacting to those old incidents." Alicia is very pulled to give the home visitor specific advice, but instead stops herself, and throws the question out to the group asking, "what is at stake here, what might need to be thought about before Trini can figure out what to do? A lively discussion follows and any time a "fix" is proposed or a member tells a story about a successful home visiting case with similar themes, Alicia, notes the power of that work, but asks the group to think about what is different in Trini's case. Alicia slows the group down repeatedly, wonders how Trini's feelings of being pulled between parent and child needs might be experienced by the family and how she can use this feeling to extend her intervention in a useful way.

Vignette 2:

Chris is an experienced facilitator working with a group of nurses in a Public Health Nursing program. Jewel, one of the more experienced nurses on the team, always proposes a solution for every difficult case presented in the group in a way that tends to cut off discussion. Patty, Jewel's team mate, is presenting one of her cases today. Chris starts by stating that when a case is similar to one we have worked with, it often seems that we know just what to do, but moving too quickly can lead us down the wrong path. He says: "Let's listen to Patty's case dilemma today and I want each of you to write down what you think she should do. We won't share these yet. Then let's each ask Patty at least one question to get a fuller picture." Then let's write again what we think she could do. Towards the end of the session, Chris asks Patty for a summary of what she has learned from the discussion, and then asks the other members if what they wrote before the discussion was different from what they wrote after they had gone into more detail.

When we repeat back what we have heard from an individual in a group to check if we have heard correctly, it demonstrates listening carefully and also offers the participant an opportunity to add or clarify. A facilitator can also check by saying, "What I heard you say is...", and maybe even add a few questions about the tone, or parts of the statement that they were not sure you understood. In this follow-up commenting and questioning it is important that there is not a tone of judgment, or argument which will tend to shut down the conversation. In Vignette 2 on page 44, the facilitator uses a simple exercise to illustrate how additional information can impact the way we move forward with a situation.

Asking Permission to Clarify

For any statement, but particularly when a statement is vague, overly general or seemingly biased in a certain direction, the facilitator can ask for clarification, or ask the other members if there is any part of what has been said that they would like expanded or clarified.

"Wonder is the beginning of wisdom" — **Socrates**

Curiosity is King

In a group, a facilitator models both curiosity and prompts others to wonder, to bring forward their perspectives, to ask questions that get at motivations, and feelings and layers of meaning. Naming that looking at a situation from various perspectives can be really helpful in building more understanding or unraveling a dilemma underscores the value of the group's questions and comments.

The Reflective Facilitator is a Conductor and the Participants Make the Music

One visual metaphor for a reflective practice group facilitator is as an orchestra conductor. The conductor provides structure to the group by providing direction, pacing, containment and facilitating engagement of all members rather than getting hung up with one or two participants. The reflective group facilitator uses a variety of techniques to increase awareness and move the group forward as individuals and ultimately as an ensemble. Like an orchestra, reflective practice groups have unique instruments and performers. Some like a timpani are more forceful, others more subtle like a piccolo, some are occasionally misattuned or a beat or two behind or ahead, but each brings something unique and essential. The conductor listens deeply, leans in, and calls in different "instruments" to create a unique version that shows the power and subtlety of the music. While a reflective practice group facilitator may naturally gravitate towards certain participants, they should acknowledge the value in every member. They may find it beneficial to engage in their own reflective consultation to explore and understand these pulls. Just as a conductor draws out the best from every instrument, including those played by beginners, the facilitator fosters engagement and encourages the full expression of all participants.

Common Difficulties in Groups – When Things Go Wrong

Members in reflective practice groups are individuals who in time develop connections with other group members and the group as a whole. Yet, in spite of this groupness that usually develops, individuals arrive as themselves with their own traits and unique ways of being that intersect with the group dynamics and the interactions between the group members and the facilitator. In this guide we have stressed the importance of creating a safe, brave space and use of agreed up and well discussed guidelines, but even when these steps have been taken, there are times when the facilitator will need to step in to make sure that there is space for all members.

There are certain behaviors in groups that merit particular attention because they are common and can disrupt a whole group if not handled well. Compounding these challenges are consideration for cultural and historical influences on the group members. In addition group members can have different ways of expressing feelings, raising problems, or just listening based on their unique circumstances, cultural shaping, or experiences where they may have been oppressed, silenced, bullied,or ignored in group settings. Care should be taken particularly with marginalized group members who may have been given clear verbal and non-verbal messages over time regarding the appropriateness of various behaviors. Here are some of the potential behaviors reflective practice group facilitators should be aware of and some suggestions for how to consider and respond to these patterns.

A Focus on Engaging exclusively with the Reflective Practice Group Facilitator 1-1
One of the things that can go wrong in groups is conversations that seem to be just between two people, instead of group conversations. This can happen when a group member seems to want the exclusive attention of the reflective practice group facilitator or to attend to them individually and the facilitator lingers in this two person exchange. Prolonged two-person exchange can also occur between group members.

When the group facilitator notices that this is happening and other group members are restless or annoyed, it is an important moment to take charge where others can be invited into the group to comment on a topic. For example:

"I am going to ask you to pause for a minute so we can ask some questions to make sure your dilemma with this grandparent is understood."

"I would love to hear some additional points of view on what you have just said so we can think together with the rest of the group about your dilemma."

Another approach when this starts to happen is for the reflective group facilitator to comment on the process, and invite others in. For example,

"I was so taken in by this story that I have been asking all the questions, but I want to step back now so we can hear your questions."

Excessive Talking

Some group members may feel compelled to talk frequently and to fill any silence immediately. The content that is shared could vary from the unnecessarily detailed and apparently irrelevant to regularly presenting dramatic stories of major crises. Initially, group members may welcome this as a way to avoid having to fill the time themselves or they may feel like this person's experience deserves more attention than what they could bring to the table. Either way, this type of behavior and resulting unresolved tension may eventually lead to a sense of divisiveness in the group. Members may drop out, miss meetings, or passively endure the meeting. If left unaddressed by the reflective practice group facilitator, a group member may finally aggressively confront the over-talking member, which may lead this person to withdraw for a few weeks or leave the group.

The facilitator can interrupt the person and prompt the participation of others perhaps even evoking the communication guidelines, but this does not always work. If the facilitator is too direct in silencing the overtalking group member, others may be deterred from speaking up themselves. Another approach could be to consider the person monopolizing the conversation and the group that has allowed itself to be monopolized. In that way, both dynamics can be addressed.

Instead of focusing on the overtalking group member, the facilitator may wonder why the group permits or encourages one member to *carry the burden of the entire meeting.* This reframing of the behavior allows both the person monopolizing the group as well as the group members to consider the function of this behavior. Could the person speaking excessively be feeling a sense of anxiety or responsibility in filling up the time in the group? Where might this be coming from? The facilitator's goal here is not to silence the group member but rather to help them notice that this behavior, while on the surface, suggests an interest in self-disclosure and engagement, actually serves to shield, entertain, or gain attention, thus keeping the group at arm's length.

Conversely, could members of the group appreciate avoiding their own self disclosures by allowing this member to take up all the space? Could this be in service of avoiding the group's attention on them? Could group members be secretly enjoying watching the group's reaction to that person? Might they like being in the position of being wronged? This type of discussion offers fertile ground in understanding our own interpersonal challenges and how they might show up in the work.

Silence

While on the surface silence or a partial disconnected presence seems like the opposite of excessive talking, there are many similarities regarding motivation and risks if not addressed. It is possible for a group member to benefit from the group consultation experience without talking; however, research on group behavior suggests that group members are more likely to benefit if they are actively engaged. There are many possible causes of the silence: group members may dread self-disclosure; they may fear appearing incompetent or being criticized about their work or prefer to maintain control by not revealing themselves. Some may be too uncomfortable to speak their mind about an issue or fear being put on the spot or asked to represent a particular point of view because of their cultural or other identity. Some are looking for permission and encouragement from the facilitator before they can speak. Some members may only speak in the absence of specific group members. Some group members may have had experiences where dominant groups in our cultures have implicitly and explicitly communicated about the value of what they have to say, expectations around when to speak, and when to remain silent. The group facilitator needs to remain aware and curious about the meaning of silence and avoid any pulls to inadvertently reinforce the silence. The challenge for the group facilitator is to attempt to draw the silent member in without placing undue pressure on them.

Micro-affirmations occur when the group facilitator or other group members positively remark on a comment or even a facial expression shared by the usually silent member. "Your comment about the grandfather's role in the family is so helpful in getting a fuller picture of this little boy's experience."

Overregulated Behavior
Some group members are very weary or sometimes very wary of emotions and choose to focus what they share on details that lack the expression of any felt emotions on their part or even on the imagined or observed emotions of others. They tend to be inhibited and lack spontaneity and refuse to take risks. Sometimes this suppression of emotions is a result of worries about rejection, beliefs that emotions need to be checked at the door, or a discomfort with focusing attention on the self. Here again the group facilitator needs to take an inquisitive stance paying close attention to their own countertransference. What about what this person is sharing is uninteresting or seems flat or incomplete? Are there times when they seem more or less inhibited? Because inhibited or overregulated behavior is generally more tolerated by other group members, no immediate action is required on the part of the facilitator other than close attention to the process. An understanding of the obstacles that might be in the way of the person's ability to unleash the creative parts of themselves can assist the facilitator to open space in ways that can allow a more complete description of a situation.

Complaining
A particularly challenging behavioral pattern that could be observed in a group is that of an individual group member who repeatedly rejects and complains about any perspectives or ideas brought forward by other group members. These group members explicitly request the group's assistance, but discount, or outwardly reject any thoughts that are offered. These responses can take many forms: sometimes it is a direct verbal rejection, e.g. "I've tried that and it did not work", or some kind of discounting statement such as," That would never work on my team."

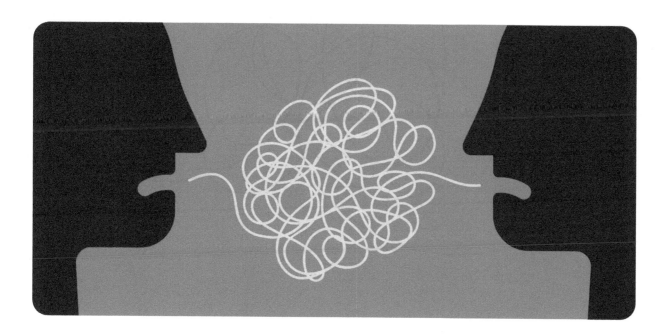

The message communicated is that this individual's problems are much more complex than anyone else's in the group. This behavior can be interpreted to be a result of conflicting feelings: on the one hand needing and depending on others and on the other hand feeling hopeless, perhaps distrusting or even resenting those offering support. If the facilitator can acknowledge the pain that one might find oneself in, the longing to be cared for and helped and simultaneously being unable to use the help offered or not getting offered the help they hoped for, it might put words to the group member's felt experience and reduce some of the tension in the group. A non-blaming, non-faulting compassionate stance is critical here.

Complaints about administrators, policies or co-workers can also take on a circular, angry or hopeless tone. These can be broad remarks about administrative or systemic issues such as, "Nobody in administration really cares about what we need to do our job," to remarks about a particular person. These behaviors fall on a continuum with some only exhibiting it in moments of great distress while others lean heavily on this pattern in interacting with their peers.

The reflective group facilitator can raise questions about avenues that are available to discuss these issues with those in charge. They can wonder about past experiences with linking staff needs to administrative concerns. It is important that reflective practice facilitators are sensitive to the experiences of participants, working to explore their experiences and felt experience with them and strengthen their abilities to bring concerns to the right people. It will also be important that the group's intention is focused on the original intent. With a group's permission, the group reflective supervisor can bring broad concerns back to an administrative team and recommend a meeting to better understand the concerns of an individual or a group.

Groupthink
Social psychologists describe groupthink as a process in a group when critical thinking or questions or dissent are suppressed out of a desire for harmony, cohesiveness, closure or closeness that often results in an irrational or dysfunctional ways of making decisions (Janus, 1984). The concept of groupthink has been widely considered and is often applied to political decision making, but the idea is important in any group situation.

When groupthink is present, exploration of a topic is usually shallow and heads in one direction leading to a kind of premature foreclosure or consensus without a full consideration of the issue. Pressures for groupthink can be present when group members may not understand, or appreciate the value of different perspectives, where members feel the implicit or explicit bias and the cost of presenting another perspective is too high, exposing, or just not worth the effort. Often groupthink is present when members have not experienced a genuine sense of collaboration and inclusiveness in current or prior settings. Considerations of why some members may be less comfortable bringing forward ideas are important. Bilingual participants may have some difficulty finding ideas in the dominant language, power differentials real and perceived may be present, past experiences in groups of being put down, ignored, or put on the spot may shape responses.

The reflective practice group facilitator's stance in addressing groupthink, is first to consider any pressures they as a leader might inadvertently be exerting in this direction, e.g. too great a sense of being the great leader, too many positive examples from their own work, a tendency to underscore and advance ideas that fit with their world view. Secondly the group facilitator should consider the experience and the situation of the participants in the group, the make-up of the group and what their own role and identities might represent to the group currently or in the past.

Lastly, the group facilitator's stance related to groupthink is to slow things down, notice the group's process, and use a stance of curiosity and openness to bring alternative thoughts, feelings, and information to an area of discussion.

Breaches of Agreements

Solid group agreements regarding confidentiality, attention to power and privilege, sharing airtime, communication about attendance, pre-discussed topics should be noticed and wondered about. Sometimes this may require a one-on-one discussion with a group member, or at times it can be important for the provider to bring the concern to the group for discussion.

If breeches are not addressed, group members can come to question the reliability of the group as a safe container for their experiences, feelings, and needs.

Group Ruptures and Possibilities for Repair

An important aspect of working with groups is the consideration of when group norms are broken, or trust is eroded by the action of the group member or facilitator, for example a micro aggression that occurs around race, culture, equity or inclusion. Sometimes ruptures happen very fast and the person causing the rupture may not even notice that they have offended or broken an agreed upon norm. Sometimes the facilitator may miss a rupture but may notice a shift in the group or a change within an individual. Ruptures can simmer, sometimes the person who feels the rupture speaks up right away, but in many cases they do not. In some cases noticing or wondering about a possible or clearly evident rupture, can be enough to cause the other person or individuals to catch themselves, apologize, or ask more about what they said or did that made others feel uncomfortable. Sometimes ruptures are missed by a facilitator and may get brought up by a group member.

Sometimes, a comment or statement will be made that a group member will take personally, as if it were directed specifically to them. This kind of personalization is often a root cause of misunderstanding, and racial tension. Questions or assumptions about differences that are too direct, ill-timed or premature can be distressing and threatening to one's image or sense of safety and can cause a reaction when a spotlight is shined prematurely on the uncomfortable.

Example 3.8 Group Rupture Vignettes

Vignette 1:

It is a group meeting between the developmental staff and the local Part C program. The group is doing an introduction and a Latinx staff member introduces herself without going into any cultural or ethnic affiliation. The program coordinator decides to go further and adds that the person is Latinx, grew up in Columbia, and speaks Spanish with a unique accent. The staff person gets very upset, and takes it personally. The program coordinator does not understand why the person is upset with her. When asked later, the staff member explained she was upset because she did not feel like it was the coordinator's right to speak about her ethnicity to the group. She felt like she was being "showcased" for her ethnicity rather than her skills.

Vignette 2:

In a reflective practice supervision group, one of the members tells a newly hired supervisor that mainly the program works with homeless clients and they are almost always Black or Brown. Helena bristles at this generalization and the failure to see people as individuals, and says in a clipped tone, "Not all our families are Black or Brown, and anybody can become homeless." Sensing how this has landed, Elena, the reflective practice facilitator says, "You are right and I sense that stating it the way I did seemed like I was really leaning into stereotypes."

Vignette 3:

In a reflective practice group Angela tells the group that she is so angry because she feels that the director is always pulling her into meetings, enlisting her because she is Black. She says: "The reality is that I am just about the only one, and rather than showing me off, we should be working harder to diversity our staff." The facilitator listens, empathizes and in time wonders out loud if anyone has any questions. In this discussion it surfaces that Angela has not "dared" to talk to the director about this and has been seething for months. The group with the help of the facilitator explore why this is so troubling to her and her reluctance to approach her director.

Often, many of the issues addressed in these vignettes are about the way that the facilitator uses negative capability or inhibits (holds back) without judging or correcting. Thus, the facilitator creates safety by taking time to explore what occurred while engaging other participants in the process and inviting a deeper exploration of a rupture. Time and space is essential, allowing for an internal dialog between the personal self and the professional self of the person who is experiencing the rupture. Time and space may allow the individuals involved in the rupture an opportunity to hear and stay regulated even when something is disturbing. That allows time for the person bringing the concern to develop more self awareness. In not moving too quickly into problem solving, the facilitator open a process for possible repair.

Repair is contingent upon the willingness of the individuals involved in the rupture to engage in a process of working through the emotions that triggered the rupture. Repair is a process that sometimes takes more time, but by delving into the rupture, the trust between the individuals and within the group can be rebuilt. It is important to re-establish the group members' feelings of safety, However, repair is the beginning of a healing process, and it happens over time and may not occur as quickly as one would like.

The facilitator's role during the process of rupture and repair is to hold the group process. They need to stick with it, remain courageous and not take sides. Remaining neutral may lead to greater awareness and being able to reflect on one's inner peacemaker. Reflecting on how discord affects the facilitator is instructive and can also guide healing.

My CoLab Partners have also developed a framework for navigating ruptures and repairs that can guide groups and individuals to address and repair ruptures through a thoughtful process. See Appendix 10: Framework and Supporting Documents.

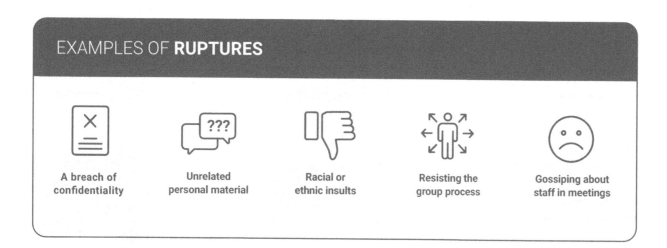

EXAMPLES OF **RUPTURES**

| A breach of confidentiality | Unrelated personal material | Racial or ethnic insults | Resisting the group process | Gossiping about staff in meetings |

Different Types of Ruptures
Using the material above, how might you address:

- A breach of confidentiality when a group member shares information about another's actions in the group.

- When an individual persistently brings in personal material not related to the intention of the group.

- A racial or ethnic insult, such as expressed disgust about a food item another member is eating.

- When an individual resists the group process, by changing the topic, reverting to their pet issue, or dismissing or diminishing views of others,

- Gossiping about a staff or administrator to the whole group.

In some cases it may be advisable to speak privately with a group member outside the group and untangle what has happened and what might be possible in terms of a repair or reconnection.

For reflective practice group facilitators it is usually best to address a difficulty about the process of the group or content expressed in the moment in a way that is not confrontational or embarrassing to the speaker, but makes it clear that you are directing the group to comment, ask questions, or bring in new perspectives. When this process occurs it is often possible to prevent or lessen a rupture.

Example 3.9 Addressing Group Process Difficulties

> *"Carl, I hear your frustration, but let's focus on the case you brought. "All those Latinx dads" is just too broad and takes us away from the particular struggle going on with this dad."*
>
> *"I know you have so much to explain about this situation, but I see that some others are dying to jump in with a question."*
>
> *"The time crunch is so real with these court cases, but we're lost in the process here, and the stuff you wanted to talk about with the family seems to have vanished, I hope we get back to them."*
>
> *"Eva, let's take a breath, it is so overwhelming to discover how frightening the aunt can be to these kids."*
>
> *"I am going to stop you here, as I want to hear another perspective about this action that seems so necessary to you."*

In groups that are comfortable with one another, group members often bring in these kinds of questions or requests for a turn in the process.

Refocusing, Understanding, and Addressing Group Malfunctions

A basic premise in working with groups is that there will often be difficult situations, missteps, omissions, and difficulties that occur in the group dynamics. Reflective practice group facilitators are not infallible and group members come with a variety of experiences, pressures, concerns, possibilities to grow, and needs. Working to understand and respond to these individual differences thoughtfully while time-consuming, often leads to groups that work more effectively to accomplish their stated purpose. This attention and recalibration of effort provides a template for the way that the participants can approach their work, e.g. with reflection, time, and experimentation with approaching a concern from many angles.

What is happening in a group that is misfiring requires consideration of the basic makeup of the group, and a consideration of the meaning of the dynamics that are present. Critical self-awareness and a willingness to look clearly at what has happened with this kind of self-awareness is central.

Here are some questions to consider as you consider difficulties. Consultation with a supervisor, mentor or trusted peer who is not a member of the group is advised.

FACILITATOR SELF-CHECKLIST

? Is the group sanctioned and supported by the participants' agencies?

? Has the purpose of the group been discussed with group members and clarified as needed by the facilitator?

? Have I as the facilitator worked to engage all members or do I tend to look to certain members more, leaving others out or minimizing their contributions?

? Are extended 1-1 conversations between groups members expanded by me to include other group members?

? Do I use the group agreements to prompt participants to do things like share airtime or point out comments that are divisive or biased in a particular way?

? Have I noticed tensions, cliques or particular divides in the group that needs to be considered and perhaps noticed and wondered about with group members?

? Have I been aware and able to address ruptures or distressing incidents in the group?

? Does the group habitually lack structure indicated by always starting late or running over time?

? Do I give myself enough time to prepare for the group using the ARC as a kind of a guide to provide a sense of structure and predictability?

? Am I able to refocus, recalibrate and proceed when things have gone off trail?

Example 3.10 Refocusing when things go wrong

A small Reflective Practice Group is meeting monthly. All the individuals are from different human service agencies and all are working at some level of leadership within their organizations. Their agencies are committed to investing in Reflective Supervision for all staff in their respective organizations. One of the participating supervisors uses the group to repeatedly vent her frustrations about the organizational infrastructure of her program and is so angry that she has difficulty listening to questions or feedback from her peers and the facilitator. The facilitator picks up on the unspoken annoyance of the other participants who are more able to move into discussing common concerns about how they are implementing reflective supervision in their agencies. The facilitator feels that if the participant who is so frustrated and angry could sink into these kinds of conversations she too might find a path forward.

Prior to the next session the facilitator reflects about where her own frustration is coming from and considers her worries about how this particular participant is impacting the group as a whole. She considers what she can do to manage her own irritation so she can more effectively help the struggling and angry participant. After realizing that her own frustration with the participant's repetitive complaints have made it hard to really hear her, she decides to set up a time to speak with the participant outside of the group to individually explore the participant's frustration. She hopes that as she holds, listens and better understands the participants' concerns, she will be able to gently approach ways she can use the group time to support new strategies and ideas. Together in the meeting they spend some time exploring the situation more fully, they jointly develop a way to contain the venting of anger during the group so that the participant can use the time and the support of other group members to move into exploring and considering strategies related to her program.

Don't Go It Alone. Consultation, Supervision and Support for Reflective Practice Group Facilitators

Group reflective practice groups of all kinds are a powerful practice that have enormous potential to support, connect, tackle individual and system problems, educate, expand, and grow the reflective functioning capacities of the members and their abilities to work more effectively with diverse populations. Facilitating reflective practice groups can be challenging at times and veteran reflective group facilitators as well as beginners benefit from and deserve the time with and assistance from others to address particular situations and obtain support to continue to build and deepen skills to provide this complicated and essential work.

It is natural to question one's judgment, to second guess, and to experience a misstep as a facilitator. The nature of groups, the difficulty of the content they may wish to discuss, issues of transference and countertransference in groups, and the fact that tensions in programs, and among colleagues can come to the group too, make it certain that all reflective group facilitators will have moments when they will benefit from a supervisor and/or a group of supportive colleagues who can help them think and feel through tricky situations that they are facilitating. This support can come in many forms: groups offered by an agency or system or individual consultation with someone with expertise in this area or community of practice groups where peers can give and obtain support. This support can offer both a chance to reflect and grow, and also an opportunity in this process to be held, to practice self compassion, and to receive what a facilitator so generously offers to others.

Online Resources – Section 3

 Facilitation Tips | Reflective Practice Facilitator tips

 21 Mindfulness Exercises & Activities For Adults (+ PDF)

 13.1 Understanding Small Groups – Communication in the Real World

 Mindfulness for Racial Justice | Taking Charge of Your Health & Wellbeing

 Groupthink | Understanding the Impact of Group Dynamics in Decision Making

 Tool: Interrupting Microaggressions

 Mindfulness Exercises

 How Microaggressions are Like Mosquito Bites • Same Difference

 A 12-Minute Medication for Challenging Emotions

 Racial Healing Self-Care Mindfulness Exercise

BIBLIOGRAPHY

Albritton, K., Mathews, R. & Anhalt, K. (2019). Systematic review of early childhood mental health consultation: Implications for improving preschool discipline disproportionality. *Journal of Educational & Psychological Consultation, 29*(4), 444–472.

Arao, B. & Clemons, K. (2013). From safe spaces to brave spaces: A new way to frame dialogue around diversity and social justice. In L. Landreman (Ed.), *The art of effective facilitation: Reflections from social justice educators* (pp.135–150). Stylus. *https://www.anselm.edu/sites/default/files/Documents/Center%20for%20Teaching%20Excellence/From%20Safe%20Spaces%20to%20Brave%20Spaces.pdf*

Barron, C. (2019). *A qualitative study of reflective supervision from the supervisee perspective: An ecological view.* Doctoral dissertations, Wayne State University. *https://digitalcommons.wayne.edu/oa_dissertations/2145*

Benbassat, N. (2020). Reflective function: A move to the level of concern. *Theory and Psychology 2020, vol. 30*(5), 657–653.

Bernstein, V. & Edwards, R. (2012). Support early childhood practitioners through relationship based, reflective supervision. *NHSA Dialog: A Research to Practice Journal for the Early Intervention Field, 15*(3), 236–301.

Bion, W. (1968). *Experiences in groups and other papers.* Routledge.

Burkhardt T., Huang L.A., Herriott A., Pacheco-Applegate A. & Spielberger J. (2023). Strengthening home visitor practice through an embedded model of infant and early childhood mental health consultation. *Prevention Science, Jan;24*(1):105–114. *https://doi.org/10.1007/s11121-022-01461-6*

Butler, L., Carello, J. & Maguin, E. (2017). Trauma, stress, and self-care in clinical training: Predictors of burnout, decline in health status, secondary traumatic stress symptoms, and compassion satisfaction. *Psychological Trauma: Theory, Research, Practice, and Policy, 9*(4), 416–424. *https://doi.org/10.1037/tra0000187*

Caplan, G. (1970). *The theory and practice of consultation.* Basic Books.

Clark, R., Gehl, M., Heffron, M., Kerr, M., Soliman, S., Shahmoon-Shanok, R. & Thomas, K. (2019). Mindful practices to enhance diversity-informed reflective supervision and leadership. *Zero to Three.*

Center of Excellence for Infant and Early Childhood Mental Health Consultation. (2021). *Annotated Bibliography: The Evidence Base for Infant and Early Childhood Mental Health Consultation (IECMHC).* *http://www.iecmhc.org/documents/CoE-Annotated-Bibliography.pdf*

Cooperrider, D. & Whitney, D. (2005). *Appreciative inquiry: A positive revolution.* Berrett-Koehler Publishers.

Davidson, N., Major, C. & Michaelsen, L. (2014). Small-group learning in higher education—cooperative, collaborative, problem-based, and team-based learning: An introduction by the guest editors. *Journal on Excellence in College Teaching, 25*(3&4), 1–6.

Dewey, J. (1910). *How we think.* D.C. Heath and Company.

Eaves Simpson, T. (2019). *Workplace supports in the infant mental health field: A mixed methods investigation.* Doctoral dissertations. *https://opencommons.uconn.edu/dissertations/2213*

Falender, C., Shafranske, E. & Falicov, C. (Eds.). (2014). *Multiculturalism and diversity in clinical supervision: A competency-based approach.* American Psychological Association. *https://doi.org/10.1037/14370-000*

Falicov, C. (1995). Training to think culturally: A multidimensional comparative framework. *Family Process 34*, 373–388.

Fenichel, E. (Ed) (1992). Learning through supervision and mentorship to support the development of infants, toddlers, and their families: a source book. *Zero to Three, National Center for Infants, Toddlers and Families.*

Fitzgibbons, S., Smith, M. & McCormick, A. (2018). Use of the reflective supervisory relationship to navigate trauma, separation, loss, and inequity on behalf of babies and their families. *ZERO TO THREE, 39*(1), 74–82.

Fonagy, P., Steele, M., Steele, H., Moran, G. & Higgitt, A. (1991). The capacity for understanding mental states: The reflective self in parent and child and its significance for security of attachment. *Infant Mental Health Journal, 12*(3), 201–218. *https://doi.org/10.1002/1097-0355(199123)12:3<201::AID-IMHJ2280120307>3.0.CO;2-7*

Gibbs, G. (1988). *Learning by doing: A guide to teaching and learning methods.* FEU.

Gilkerson, L. & Heffron, M. (2015). *FAN Arc.* Erikson Institute.

Hardy, K. & Bobes, T. (Eds) (2015). *Promoting cultural sensitivity in supervision: A manual for practitioners.* Routledge.

Harrell, S. (2014). Compassionate confrontation and empathic exploration: The Integration of race narratives in clinical supervision. In C. Falender, E. Shafranske & C. Falicov (Eds). *Multiculturalism and diversity in clinical supervision: A competency-based approach.* (pp. 83–110). American Psychological Association. ***https://doi.org/10.1037/14370-004***

Heffron, M., Reynolds, D. & Talbot, B. (2016). Reflecting together: Reflective functioning as a focus for deepening group supervision. *Infant Mental Health Journal, 37,* 628–639.

Ixer, G. (2016). The concept of reflection: Is it skill based or values? *Social Work Education, 35*(7), 809–824. ***http://dx.doi.org/10.1080/02615479.2016.1193136***

Janis, I. (1982). *Groupthink: Psychological studies of policy decisions and fiascos.* Houghton Mifflin.

Johns, C. (2022). *Becoming a reflective practitioner. (6th ed.).* Wiley.

Kabat-Zinn, J. (2013). *Full catastrophe living. Using the wisdom of your body and mind to face stress, pain, and illness. (2nd ed.).* Bantam Books.

Knight, K., Sperlinger, D. & Maltby, M. (2010). Exploring the personal and professional impact of reflective practice groups: A survey of 18 cohorts from a UK clinical psychology training course. *Clinical Psychology & Psychotherapy, 17,* 427–437.

Kornfield, J. (1993). *A path with heart: a guide through the perils and promises of spiritual life.* Bantam Books.

Kurtz, A. (2020). *How to run reflective practice groups.* Routledge.

Lingras, K. (2022). Mind the Gap(s): Reflective supervision/consultation as a mechanism for addressing implicit bias and reducing our knowledge gaps. *Infant Mental Health Journal, Jul;43*(4):638-652. ***https://doi.org/10.1002/imhj.21993***

Luyten, P., Mayes, L., Nijssens, L. & Fonagy, P. (2017). The parental reflective functioning questionnaire: Development and preliminary validation. *PLoS One, May;12*(5): e0176218. ***https://doi.org/10.1371/journal.pone.0176218***

Magee, R. (2019). *The inner work of racial justice: Healing ourselves and transforming our communities through mindfulness.* TarcherPerigee.

Menekem, R. (2017). *My grandmother's hands: Racialized trauma and the paths to mending our hearts and bodies.* Recovery Press.

National Council on Crime and Delinquency (2006). *Relationship between staff turnover, child welfare system functioning and recurrent child abuse.* National Council on Crime and Delinquency.

Patel, R. (2015). *The role of reflective practice in educating about race, identity and difference.* Doctoral dissertation, Manchester Metropolitan University

Porges, S. (2020). The covid-19 pandemic is a paradoxical challenge to our nervous system: a polyvagal perspective. *Clinical Neuropsychiatry.* Apr;17(2), 135–138. ***https://doi.org/10.36131/CN20200220***

Pranis, K. (2005). *The little book of circle processes: A new/old approach to peacemaking.* Good Books.

Priddis, L. & Rogers S. (2017). Development of the reflective practice questionnaire: preliminary findings. *Reflective Practice, 19*(1), 89–104. ***https://doi.org/10.1080/14623943.2017.1379384***

Proctor, B. (2008). *Group supervision: A guide for creative practice. (2nd ed.).* Sage Publications.

Schechter, D., Coots, T., Zeanah, C., Davies, M., Coates, S., Trabka, K., Marshall, R., Liebowitz, M., & Myers, M. (2005). Maternal mental representations of the child in an inner-city clinical sample: Violence-related posttraumatic stress and reflective functioning. *Attachment and Human Development, Sep;7*(3), 313–31. ***https://doi.org/10.1080/14616730500246011***

Schon, D. (1991). *The reflective practitioner.* Ashgate Publishing.

Shapiro, S., Astin, J., Bishop, S. & Cordova, M. (2005). Mindfulness based stress reduction for health care professionals: Results from a randomized trial. *International Journal of Stress Management, 12*(2), 164–176.

Shivers, E., Faragó, F. & Gal-Szabo, D. (2021). The role of infant and early childhood mental health consultation in reducing racial and gender relational and discipline disparities between Black and white preschoolers. *Psychology in the Schools, 59*(10), 1965-1983. ***https://doi.org/10.1002/pits.22573***

Silverman, M. & Hutchinson, B. (2019). Reflective capacity: An antidote to structural racism cultivated through mental health consultation. *Infant Mental Health Journal, 40*(5), 742–756. ***https://doi.org/10.1002/imhj.21807***

Slade, A., Sadler, L. & Mayes, L. (2005). *Minding the Baby®: Enhancing parental reflective functioning and infant attachment in a nursing / mental health home visiting program.* In Berlin, L.J., Ziv, Y., Amaya Jackson, L. & Greenberg, M.T. (Eds), *Enhancing early attachments: theory, research, intervention, and policy* (pp. 152–177). Guilford Press.

Steele, H., Murphy, A., Bonuck, K., Meissner, P. & Steele, M. (2019). Randomized control trial report on the effectiveness of Group Attachment-Based Intervention (GABI®): Improvements in the parent-child relationship not seen in the control group. *Development and Psychopathology, 31*(1), 203–217. ***https://doi.org/10.1017/S0954579418001621***

Suchman, N., DeCoste, C., McMahon, T., Dalton, R., Mayes, L. & Borelli, J. (2017). Mothering From the Inside Out: Results of a second randomized clinical trial testing a mentalization-based intervention for mothers in addiction treatment. *Development and Psychopathology, 29*(2), 617–636. ***https://doi.org/10.1017/S0954579417000220***.

Sue, D., Alsaidi, S., Awad, N., Glaeser, E., Calle, C. & Mendez, N. (2019). Disarming racial microaggressions: Microinterventions strategies for targets, white allies & bystanders. *American Psychologist, 74*(1), 128–142.

Thomas, K., Noroña, C. & St. John, M. (2019). Cross-sector allies together in the struggle for social justice Diversity-Informed Tenets for Work with Infants, Children and Families. *ZERO TO THREE, 39*(3), 44–54. ***https://www.zerotothree.org/resource/journal/cross-sector-allies-together-in-the-struggle-for-social-justice-diversity-informed-tenets-for-work-with-infants-children-and-families/***

Tuckman, B. & Jensen, M. (1977). Stages of small group development revisited. *Group and Organizational Studies, 2,* 419–427.

Turner, S. (2009). Exploring resilience in the lives of women leaders in early childhood health, human services, and education. Doctoral dissertation, Oregon State University.

Virmani, E. & Ontai, L. (2010). Supervision and training in child care: Does reflective supervision foster caregiver insightfulness? *Infant Mental Health Journal, 31*(1), 16–32.

West, A., Madariaga, P. & Sparr, M. (2022). *Reflective supervision: What we know and what we need to know to support and strengthen the home visiting workforce* (OPRE Report No. 2022–101). Office of Planning, Research, and Evaluation; Administration for Children and Families; U.S. Department of Health and Human Services.

Woltmann, E., Whitley, R., McHugo, G., Brunette, M., Torrey, W., Coots, L., Lynde, D. & Drake, R. (2008). The role of staff turnover in the implementation of evidence-based practices in mental health care. *Psychiatric Services, 59*(7), 732–737.

Yalom, I. & Leszcz, M. (2020). *The theory and practice of group psychotherapy, (6th ed.).* Basic Books.

APPENDICES

These materials have been referred to in the text and they provide samples or additional information that can be used or adapted for use in planning, running, or evaluating groups.

1. Mental Health Consultation in Child Care: The Consultative Stance

2. What is Reflection and Reflective Practice? FAQ

3. Sample Group Agreements

4. Sample Questions that Prompt Reflection in Groups

5. Engaging in Approaches that support Reflection and Collaboration

6. Group Facilitator Self-Assessment Tool

7. Tracking Content & Process in a Reflective Practice Group

8. Participants' Evaluation Form Sample

9. Measuring Reflective Supervision within Home Visiting

10. Rupture and Repair Framework

APPENDIX 1

Mental Health Consultation in Child Care –
The Consultative Stance

(Excerpted and paraphrased from Johnston, K, and Brinamen, C. (2006). Mental Health Consultation in Child Care: Transforming Relationships Among Directors, Staff, and Families (pp. 14-20). Washington, DC: ZERO TO THREE Press.)

"How you are is as important as what you do.[1]" These words, offered in the late 1990's, opened the eyes and minds of early childhood practitioners across the nation and the world. In application to the practice of consultation, this premise asserts that the power (or futility) of the consultative relationship lies in the consultant's "way of being"—the consultative stance.

10 Elements Comprise the Essential Core of an Effective Consultative Stance

1. **Mutuality of endeavor. Consultation can only be effective when the consultee contributes to and participates in the process.**

   ◆ Consultants convey the necessity of constructing hypotheses together.

   ◆ A full understanding of the situation is only possible with input from the consultee.

   ◆ The consultant's advice being "right" is useless if it does not consider the caregiver's perspective and understanding of the situation and, ultimately, the caregiver's willingness to participate in bringing about change.

2. **Avoiding the position of sole expert. In accepting that the work is a collaborative effort between consultant and providers and parents, the expert stance must be abandoned.**

   ◆ Consultant does have crucial knowledge...

   ◆ However, gathering information from all participants is critical.

   ◆ Consultant seeks to legitimize and heighten provider's own sense of expertise.

   ◆ Consultant attitude conveys belief that providers hold valuable ideas, therefore they see themselves as the source of ideas.

   ◆ Avoiding the position of expert becomes increasingly difficult when called in to respond to a crisis.

3. **Wondering instead of knowing. "Wondering with, not acting upon[2]" the caregivers with whom we**

   ◆ Are consulting elicits their involvement in the process and properly preserves the sense of the consultee as the holder of essential information and knowledge and as the agent of change.

   ◆ The consultant's stance of wondering, not knowing, demonstrates that understanding is a process, not a moment.

   ◆ Understanding the caregiver's subjective experience of the child is essential.

   ◆ Wondering, instead of "knowing the right response," holds benefits:

   ◆ The complexities of the situation can be understood, and the response can consider the needs of the child as well as the adults in the room.

---

[1] Pawl, J. H. & St. John, M. (1998). *How you are is as important as what you do... in making a positive difference for infants, toddlers, and their families.* Washington DC: Zero to Three/National Center for Infants, Toddlers, and Families.

[2] Pawl, J. (1997). Personal communication with the author.

- The caregiver has the experience of participating in the solution, allowing confidence in her ability to effect change.

- The consultant instills the idea that relationships affect children's behavior, that patience is a response, and that "not knowing" is not incompetence, but an experience that precedes understanding.

- Understanding another's subjective experience. The consultant introduces the importance of "not knowing" by demonstrating curiosity about the internal experience of the other.

- The caregiver's understanding of the child as well as herself is as crucial to creating change as any expertise either party might possess.

4. **Full understanding might require exploration of the caregiver's history and experiences of parenting and childhood to uncover obstacles to employing knowledge that a provider possesses.**

5. **Considering all levels of influence. In addition to the personal histories of child-care providers, there are numerous other influences on their views of a child and their ability to respond effectively.**

   - Some are internal

   - Many are external (programmatic pressures, program philosophies)

   - Interpersonal relationships with co-workers, administrators, and parents influence the provider's perception of and interaction with children.

   - The provider-child relationship cannot be meaningfully considered or addressed separately from the many systems within which it exists.

6. **"Hearing and representing all voices[3]"—especially the child's. Eliciting the voices of all child care community members, the consultant is dedicated to hearing about and from each individual.**

   - The consultant demonstrates that various views can be held and heard equally.

   - When necessary, the consultant represents the perspective of one participant to another with the aim of increasing the adult's capacity to and belief in the usefulness of communicating directly to one another.

   - The goal is not to negotiate a particular outcome, but to enlist cooperation among those involved in children's lives.

   - The consultant gives voice to those with no words—the children.

7. **The centrality of relationships. Because we know that development is transactional and mental health is promoted through interactions between child and caregivers, the centrality of relationships underlies all of our beliefs about consultation.**

   - Understanding caregivers' subjective experiences and giving voice to children's experiences helps the consultant to realize fully the complexities of the relationships and interactions.

   - For development to proceed smoothly, the adult relationships surrounding the child must be interlocked.

---

[3] Pawl, J. (2000). The interpersonal center of the work that we do. In Responding to infants and parents: Inclusive interaction in assessment, consultation, and treatment in infant/family practice (pp.5-7). Washington, DC: ZERO TO THREE: National

8. **Parallel process as an organizing principle. The consultant's way of being emanates from her conviction that the ways in which people are treated affect how they will feel about themselves and treat other people.**

   ◆ "Do unto others as you would have others do unto others.[4]"

   ◆ As the consultant respects, values, and seeks to understand the consultee, the caregiver in turn becomes better able to respect, value, and empathize with the experiences of the children.

9. **Patience. Just as we encourage and attempt to foster patience in caregivers' relationships with children, we must also be patient with the child-care providers and parents.**

   ◆ Sometimes it is necessary that we focus on the future children in the care of the provider, not exclusively on the children currently in the program.

   ◆ Understanding that current functioning emerges from the history of all participants in the relationship, we must understand the challenges in changing perceptions and related actions.

10. **Holding hope. Child care providers often lose hope in the face of daily crises and persistent challenges.**

   ◆ The consultant must maintain her belief in change in a slowly shifting system.

   ◆ The consultant can also hold hope for the child care providers and parents, because she is the only one that regularly has the luxury of stepping out of the seemingly static system to see the possibilities.

---

[4] *Pawl, J. H. & St. John, M. (1998). How you are is as important as what you do... in making a positive difference for infants, toddlers, and their families. Washington DC: Zero to Three/National Center for Infants, Toddlers, and Families.*

APPENDIX 2

What is Reflection and Reflective Practice? FAQ

Reflection is the active process of stepping back to look at our own experiences and those of others in order to make meaning.

Why do we use the term reflective practice, not just say reflection?
Reflective practice involves having a routine and regular time to reflect about our work. It is considered a "best practice" and has been shown to improve program quality in many studies. It has also been shown to reduce burnout, secondary traumatization, and compassion fatigue.

Isn't Reflection or Reflective Practice overthinking or navel gazing?
Reflective Practice helps us choose the best professional actions in the moment. If we don't use reflection, we often do not consider an action fully and may make more mistakes or impose our own values and ideas. Reflection is also a good skill in our personal lives.

What are the essential parts to reflective practice?

◆   Think about what happened

◆   Pay attention to feelings as well as thoughts

◆   Think about what it meant to you and how you understand

◆   Deeply consider how what happened, what might be, and what it means for somebody else; Step into their shoes

◆   Remember the things that may not be apparent or present, e.g. history of trauma, loss, cultural or regional differences, religious or moral beliefs or practices, gender or generational differences

What is the timeline for reflection?

◆   Reflecting before action, after action, and while "in action"

Why is Self-Reflection, or Critical Self Reflection so important?

◆   How we think and feel influences our behavior. Important to recognize our own patterns, preferences, and implicit and explicit biases.

◆   We want to consider for ourselves and others factors like race, power and privilege and how these can impact behavior.

◆   We want to recognize our own mental states (e.g. "that team meeting made me anxious") and also be able to think about the mental states of others. ("I wonder if she didn't come because she thinks I am judging her") so we avoid getting our exercise by jumping to conclusions.

What is the difference between reflective practice and reflective supervision?
Reflective supervision uses "reflective practice" approaches and skills, but a reflective supervisor is also responsible for program quality, and other tasks. Reflective practice is often an activity run by a program that just focuses on the work with children and families or the work with staff. . Reflective practice can also happen with peers, on your own, or informally and should always be a part of activities like reflective supervision, team meetings, management and community meetings.

What Gets in the Way of Reflective Practice?

- Judgmental thinking, " I am right, you are wrong, or uninformed"

- Seeking to blame others, or criticize them

- Our own activation or worries sometimes feeling inadequate or overwhelmed

- Assumptions about another's motivations for doing something

- Moving too quickly to acting on a problem without thinking it through

- Failure of an agency to provide staff time and support to reflect and build staff capacity, rather than relying on top down approaches only

What are the skills involved in reflective practice?

1. Slowing down and creating a ritual or routine for reflecting on one's work.

2. Stay aware of ourselves and remain receptive to the subjective experience of others.

3. In every transaction thinking of the cultural and historical contributions as well as economic and trauma-based experiences that may be shaping you and the person you are working with.

    - Considering the perspective of others who are involved and their internal emotional experience.

    - Realizing that acknowledging an experience or a way of seeing the world is not the same as approving or encouraging.

    - Considering the context, what are the rules, expectations, and patterns in a home, school or other setting.

    - Wondering and exploring staying curious

    - Reflecting rather than reacting or jumping to a conclusion about something.

    - Identifies obstacles

    - Collaborate and seek to bring out the knowledge and preferences of the other rather than take over and be an expert.

    - Learn to ask questions that encourage reflection and exploration

    - Taking time to assess rather than assume things are one way.

    - Holding hope, bearing witness

    - Regulate ourselves when there is tension or pressure.

    - Realizing that listening, exploring and being with is a profound way of helping and healing

What are some good questions to encourage reflection?

- I am not sure I understand, can you tell me a little more how that was for you in that moment?

- Is there anything in particular that you have experienced in this case that has made this parent so difficult to work with?

- What do you imagine might be happening that is causing her to reject your help?

- What comes up for you when you consider this home visitor's needs?

Developed by Mary Claire Heffron for the Capstone Facilitator's Training Program-Monterey First Five Infant and Early Childhood Mental Health Training Program

APPENDIX 3

Sample Group Agreements

Option One

Participants are given an outline like the one below. On the first meeting participants review the guidelines. The facilitator goes through them, and asks for questions, and also asks for any changes that they see are needed in the guidelines. This could be in wording or there could be other specifics that the group feels are important. These are discussed, and on the second meeting the Reflective Group Facilitator Presents the a version of the guidelines that reflects any changes that were made.

Sample Announcement:

A Home Visiting Support Group has been planned and formed to continue to build home visiting skills such as engagement and retention of clients getting medical care at participating clinics and provide ongoing support and professional development opportunities for members of the Southside Home visiting Collective which consists of programs from three participating Health Clinics. This is meant to be a space for staff to feel safe and connected that promotes collaboration. We want this space to be a place where you can be vulnerable and brave, bringing up conflicts, feelings, and concerns related to your work.

Participation is a requirement for all home visiting staff with less than 5 years of experience, and all home visitors are welcome. Please remember to sign in to the group. A calendar with group dates is printed on the backside of this document.

Each Group will begin with a short exercise to help participants shift from their work activities to participation in the group. Once the group meets, members will decide the best way to discuss their work and share the space. All groups end with a summary and a chance to reflect and think about insights, frustration, feelings and knowledge they have experienced.

Participants will meet twice a month on the first and third Wednesdays from 3:00-4:30. The group will meet for six months and then conduct an evaluation group to consider the usefulness of the group for participants. Participating staff are paid for the hours at the group.

What is discussed in the group is confidential and members are also expected to keep specific content from the group confidential. The group facilitator is Bonnie Torres LCSW. See her bio which is attached. She will provide attendance records to program directors and general information about the progress of the work, but no individual information. Participants are expected to attend groups except when ill or on vacation.

Here are the guidelines for participation for group members. These will be discussed at the first meeting and amended as necessary to address the needs and interests of the group.

1. *What is said in the group, stays in the group and confidentiality is essential. When discussing a case, please do not use identifiable names. If what is discussed impacts the direction or activities in a particular case, the group member can discuss any insights from work with the group to the individual supervisor, but should not link these changes to any particular members in the group, but rather to their reflection in the group that shifted their understanding.*

(Continued on the following page.)

(Continued from the previous page.)

2. *Ethnicity, race, culture, belief systems, spiritual/religious practices, gender, sexual identification, and other social factors are pertinent to our roles. It's crucial to recognize how historical and personal trauma, as well as disparities in access to resources such as education, housing, and emotional support, can affect our clients. Please approach each interaction with attentive listening, respect, and a willingness to understand diverse perspectives and practices.*

3. *In presenting cases and client dilemmas it will be helpful to consider the social location of yourself and clients including different perspectives, values and ways of expressing emotion and needs.*

4. *In the group please be open to the perspectives of others, and also to asking questions that help clarify what somebody has stated or question an aspect of the work.*

5. *Please be aware of any aspects of privilege and power in the group that could constrict participation of others, e.g. seniority in work, knowledge of community, language facility, roles, race, culture and gender. If you are a group member with more power, remain aware of how this can be used to further the purposes of the group.*

6. *Be aware of your style and comfort in the group and make room for all to participate. If you participate easily, be sure to step back so others can have space to talk. If group participation is less comfortable, consider taking risks to add your experiences and point of view to the discussion. The reflective practice group facilitator will be here to help with this.*

7. *Ruptures between group members may occur. At times a group member may unintentionally or even intentionally say something that is hurtful to another group member. If this occurs often, the reflective group facilitator will notice what happened, and encourage discussion. However, group members are encouraged to bring up and discuss anything that is taken as a slight, insult, or microaggression.*

Please sign here to indicate that you have read this agreement. _____
Please call if you have any questions.

Option Two
Sample Announcement:

New Message — ↗ ✕

To   John Doe   Cc Bcc

Subject   Announcing Home Visiting Support Group

A Home Visiting Support Group has been planned and formed to continue to build home visiting skills such as engagement and retention of clients getting medical care at participating clinics and provide ongoing support and professional development opportunities for members of the Southside Home visiting Collective which consists of programs from three participating Health Clinics. This is meant to be a space for staff to feel safe and connected that promotes collaboration. We want this space to be a place where you can be vulnerable and brave, bringing up conflicts, feelings, and concerns related to your work.

Participation is a requirement for all home visiting staff with less than 5 years of experience, and all home visitors are welcome. Please remember to sign in to the group. A calendar with group dates is printed on the backside of this document.

Each Group will begin with a short exercise to help participants shift from their work activities to participation in the group. Once the group meets, members will decide the best way to discuss their work and share the space. All groups end with a summary and a chance to reflect and think about insights, frustration, feelings and knowledge they have experienced.

Participants will meet twice a month on the first and third Wednesdays from 3:00-4:30. The group will meet for six months and then conduct an evaluation group to consider the usefulness of the group for participants. Participating staff are paid for the hours at the group.

What is discussed in the group is confidential and members are also expected to keep specific content from the group confidential. The group facilitator is Bonnie Torres LCSW. See her bio which is attached. She will provide attendance records to program directors and general information about the progress of the work, but no individual information. Participants are expected to attend groups except when ill or on vacation.

For the first meeting of the group the task will be to consider what guidelines will be helpful so that space can feel safe and connected and also vulnerable and brave. We will build those guidelines in our discussion, and provide a printed set that we can use through the meetings to guide us as we work together to support one another and build our professional skills and grow in awareness about our roles and what we bring to them

Send ▾

Note: This approach to group agreements is inspired by the work of Ken Hardy and Toby Bobes in their work Hardy, K. & Bobes, T. (eds). 2016 Culturally Sensitive Supervision and Training Diverse Perspectives and Practical Applications. Routledge, New York, New York.

APPENDIX 4

Sample Questions that Prompt Reflection in Groups

Observing
- I noticed our group got so very quiet when we started to talk about how to respond to a biased statement.
- I have observed that when we discuss a case, there is a hesitation to ask questions about the client's social location, I'd love to understand more about this.

Checking
- Are there things that any of you would want to add to what we have discussed about the change in that requirement?
- Does what the group is saying about this shift raise any questions or concerns?

Problem Questioning
- Is this how you all expected it would turnout?
- Is there anything any of you would question about the decision that has been made related to Johnny's placement?
- Are you as a group satisfied with the way we are headed with our parent activities?

Emotional Brainstorming
- Do you have some ideas about what he might be feeling when he's the last one to be picked up at the end of the day?
- What's your sense of what it's feeling like for that mom to be as the only Latinx Spanish speaking family in the program?

Pausing and Reviewing
- Could we take a minute and revisit what just happened?
- Might it be useful to pause and take stock of what collectively you are learning about this little boy?

Resonating
- What was that like for you individually and as a group when you found out that our director is retiring? ...
- Were there some of the different thoughts of feelings called up by what happened this week?

Perspective Taking
- Can you imagine what it's like to be four years old and your mom is a police officer?
- I wonder what it feels like to be only able to see your child in this kind of supervised setting

Visioning
- How would you all want things to change?
- Can you envision a different outcome? What would that look like?

Considering Action
- What do you think that the mother could say or do that might repair things between the grandparents?
- What are the choices that you see that this parent could explore?

Inviting Action
- What would be the first step you would be willing to take?
- Weighing Options
- Let's look at some different perspectives about the potential benefit of that change?
- Is there a down side to trying that out?

Taking A Pulse
- Do you think we are ready to move on or is more time needed?
- As we are about at the end our meeting time, would you all be willing to say a few words about how the process felt or what you are taking away with you?

Inspired by the work of Peter Fonagy 2009 and the Portage project (CESA 5 https://www.cesa5.org).

APPENDIX 5

Engaging in Approaches that Support Reflection and Collaboration

APPROACH	DESCRIPTION	EXAMPLE QUOTES
Mirroring/being with	Deeply paying attention, listening, and mirroring back the content present. Checking back if needed.	*"It seems hard to hear the details of Maria's struggles with her partner, particularly now that she is pregnant. Am I getting that accurately?"*
Reframing, looking for the feeling or circumstances under the behavior	Listening carefully and stating a view of the situation through another lens.	*"I've been listening to your case presentation and sense that you are upset with the outcome"* *"I am wondering where you feel it in your body?"*
Transforming judgements into questions	Asking a question about what is heard as a criticism or judgement sometimes helps expand perception.	*"Do you think Tania might be using her negative statements about Damien to cover up her fear that her little boy's aggression might be related to seeing his parents fighting?*
Focused Affirmation	Noticing a specific action, intervention, or shift in a case, helps supervisee feel seen and heard. Generalized affirmation can seem disingenuous.	*"Do you think Tania might be using her negative statements about Damien to cover up her fear that her little boy's aggression might be related to seeing his parents fighting?"*
Hypothesize and Invite	Raise a point of view different than the supervisee and remain genuinely open to discussion.	*"I noticed that when you offered this family a later time for the visits, they have not had any missed appointments."*
Remain Tentative	When bringing forward information state what you are talking about in a tentative way, particularly when you are missing information or the perspective of the individual.	*"I have wondered if Elena's fear of going to the follow-up appointment is related to her prior experience at the hospital? Do you think there is any possibility that is what's going on for her?"*
Promoting Critical Reflection	Supporting supervisee to look more deeply at a particular area in order to expand their self-awareness or appreciation of the client's circumstances, needs or perspectives.	*"I'm noticing that it is hard for you to get these reports on families in on time, and I am not sure if I fully get why this has been so difficult."* *"Can we take a minute to look again at this report? I wonder if there is a way to write about this family that more fully taps into their migration and adaptation history?*
Refocusing and Balancing	Holding both the supervisee's needs and the needs of the program and clients.	*"It is so important that we discuss this process of reunifying the children with the family, and I need to break in here for a moment, just to think with you about how to address the concern about the housing situation that was unclear before."*
Bearing Witness	Many times supervisees have been in the middle of difficult situations, a baby that won't stop crying, loss of a family member, interpersonal or family violence. Being available to listen and support without moving too quickly towards action steps is essential.	*"What a lot to take in, is there more that is coming up for you?"*
Slow down and double back	Often supervisee's lay out many details without reflecting on their own experience of the situation, or taking stock of the client's perspective on it.	*"Let's stop here and look back at what you have said and also want to get more of a sense of what your experience was of being with the dad and little boy in that moment."*
Bringing the mind home	Supervision encounters individually and in groups benefit from a time to invite the supervisee(s) to recalibrate by having a moment of silence, a cup of tea in silence, or a few deep breaths.	*"Before we start let's take a few minutes to slow down and center."*

These techniques are adapted from materials in Reflective Supervision and Leadership in Infant and Early Childhood Programs, Heffron, M. Murch, T. Zero to Three Press, 2010 and the Portage Project Partnering Strategies.

APPENDIX 6

Group Facilitator Self-Assessment Tool

1. I use the structure of the FAN ARC to create a routine for preparation and to structure and build collaboration in my group meetings.
   - ❑ Unfamiliar
   - ❑ Familiar; don't use
   - ❑ Use; still learning
   - ❑ Use; can explain to others

2. I am able to attune to both individuals and the whole group and use reflective questions that help participants think about a topic or a response in a more complex way.
   - ❑ Unfamiliar
   - ❑ Familiar; don't use
   - ❑ Use; still learning
   - ❑ Use; can explain to others

3. I am able to track the process and tone of the group and make descriptive comments and summarize in ways that help engage all and keep the group together.
   - ❑ Unfamiliar
   - ❑ Familiar; don't use
   - ❑ Use; still learning
   - ❑ Use; can explain to others

4. I am able to use "linking language" to encourage group members to engage with one another rather than always being at the center of exchanges.
   - ❑ Unfamiliar
   - ❑ Familiar; don't use
   - ❑ Use; still learning
   - ❑ Use; can explain to others

5. I recognize when I am dysregulated as I lead the group and know how to regulate myself so I can remain present in the group.
   - ❑ Unfamiliar
   - ❑ Familiar; don't use
   - ❑ Use; still learning
   - ❑ Use; can explain to others

6. I am able to offer a pause when the whole group seems to be activated or dysregulated.
   - ❑ Unfamiliar
   - ❑ Familiar; don't use
   - ❑ Use; still learning
   - ❑ Use; can explain to others

7. I notice and I am able to respectfully redirect an individual or the group when there is rapid movement to problem solving.
   - ❑ Unfamiliar
   - ❑ Familiar; don't use
   - ❑ Use; still learning
   - ❑ Use; can explain to others

8. I am able to invite multiple perspectives by wondering how others in the group might view an idea or by posing a question that opens up a topic in a more expansive way.
   - ❑ Unfamiliar
   - ❑ Familiar; don't use
   - ❑ Use; still learning
   - ❑ Use; can explain to others

9. I am able to notice how when a participant is dominating the discussion in a negative way and can slow down the group process and open space for others in a way that is respectful of all the group members.
   - ❑ Unfamiliar
   - ❑ Familiar; don't use
   - ❑ Use; still learning
   - ❑ Use; can explain to others

10. I use specific and accurate language rather than general praise to highlight positive insights and contributions of individuals and the group.
    - ❑ Unfamiliar
    - ❑ Familiar; don't use
    - ❑ Use; still learning
    - ❑ Use; can explain to others

11. I notice a bias or a way that one group member has presented an inaccurate or stereotyped idea and can expand the conversation in a way that does not shut down dialog or polarize the group.
    - ❑ Unfamiliar
    - ❑ Familiar; don't use
    - ❑ Use; still learning
    - ❑ Use; can explain to others

12. I acknowledge when I have made a misstep in the group and make a reparative statement out loud.
   ❏ Unfamiliar   ❏ Familiar; don't use   ❏ Use; still learning   ❏ Use; can explain to others

13. I bring in a "drop" of useful information to the group and invite exploration without dominating or taking over the process.
   ❏ Unfamiliar   ❏ Familiar; don't use   ❏ Use; still learning   ❏ Use; can explain to others

14. *I can summarize where the group is by holding onto a thread in a discussion, noting a change and checking-in to see if the group is ready to move on.*
   ❏ Unfamiliar   ❏ Familiar; don't use   ❏ Use; still learning   ❏ Use; can explain to others

15. *I can support members to reflect on and integrate material from the group discussion.*
   ❏ Unfamiliar   ❏ Familiar; don't use   ❏ Use; still learning   ❏ Use; can explain to others

Developed by Mary Claire Heffron, Tala Ghantous, Beth Reeves Fortney and Linda Gilkerson

The following are examples of the skills described in this assessment:

I notice some of us are ready to move into really finding out more about this situation, but I'd like to check in with the whole group and see what would be most useful now
What Carlos has shared is very worrisome and let's just take a few seconds to settle and take a few breathes, before we move forward.

This case example is bringing up lots of different feelings in our group and I just want to make sure we make space for everyone's ideas.

That is a very good question and I want to ask others in our group today how they might see this in their work settings.

You are bringing up one strong possibility, but I'd like us to take some time to explore a few more perspectives and ideas before we look at this in more depth.

You have brought up some key ideas here and I would love to hear if there are other perspectives that somebody wants to bring into this conversation.

We seem to be focusing a lot on the mom's needs for drug treatment and wonder if we are ready to move on to any of the other topics that we wanted to talk about...

I noticed that Carol's remark about teen parents seemed to make some of us uncomfortable. Can we take a little time here to consider how this is impacting us right now?

Wow, there are some big feelings in this group about spanking and this is a tricky topic, but I want to make sure that there is space for any other perspectives or insights about this. Let's take a second and make space for anybody who wants to add any ideas we have not discussed or who might be able to bring in helpful examples.

Luis, it is very helpful that you are sharing the specific steps needed to initiate an IEP, or Angie, your insights about what this parent has gone through are helping us all bring more empathy to this situation.

Darla, I appreciate your openness about your discomfort with male teachers based on the feedback you have from parents and I am wondering how we can think about this example in our work when we are trying to help a male colleague feel seen and valued in a preschool.

I want to acknowledge that this kind of situation is hard for me based on my involvement with parents in the prison system. I just rushed in and started to be a little bit bossy. I apologize, I really want to hear more about Cary's work before I start sharing my own experience.

APPENDIX 7

Tracking Content & Process in a Reflective Practice Group

This Form is Meant to Help Reflective Practice Facilitators Track Group Process for the Purpose of Ongoing Assessment and Improvement of Groups.

1. Facilitator introduced or reiterated the purpose of group in an engaging way for participants and reminded them of prior group agreements.

   ❑ Yes   ❑ No   ❑ Possible improvement

2. Facilitator took time to help the group come together using some kind of grounding or mindfulness process.

   ❑ Yes   ❑ No   ❑ Possible improvement

3. Facilitator was able to invite participants into some form of the work of the group.

   ❑ Yes   ❑ No   ❑ Possible improvement

4. Facilitator was able to maintain an environment where participants felt safe and also free to express a variety of perspectives.

   ❑ Yes   ❑ No   ❑ Possible improvement

5. Participants were engaged most of time.

   ❑ Yes   ❑ No   ❑ Possible improvement

6. Facilitator was able to engage most of the participants in active discussions.

   ❑ Yes   ❑ No   ❑ Possible improvement

7. Facilitator was able to use non-intrusive approaches to invite less active participants into discussion or limit participation of anyone who was dominating the conversation, or breaking one of the groups' agreements.

   ❑ Yes   ❑ No   ❑ Possible improvement

8. Facilitator was able to notice and explore statements such as micro-aggressions, implicit or explicit bias, or any name calling or labeling.

   ❑ Yes   ❑ No   ❑ Possible improvement

9. Facilitator seemed engaged and relaxed at least 50% of time.

   ❑ Yes   ❑ No   ❑ Possible improvement

10. Facilitator took time before the end of the group to allow the group to summarize their experience and takeaways from the group.

   ❑ Yes   ❑ No   ❑ Possible improvement

Facilitator's concerns and plans for next session:

APPENDIX 8

Participants Evaluation Form Sample

Please rank each statement 1 2 3 4 5 (Not at all to very much)

1. I feel that I can express a variety of perspectives and ideas in this group.
   ❑ 1　　　❑ 2　　　❑ 3　　　❑ 4　　　❑ 5

2. I can express not knowing and my vulnerability as an intervenor in this group.
   ❑ 1　　　❑ 2　　　❑ 3　　　❑ 4　　　❑ 5

3. I trust that what I say in this group remains within the group.
   ❑ 1　　　❑ 2　　　❑ 3　　　❑ 4　　　❑ 5

4. I feel it is safe to bring up experiences, questions, and a variety of perspectives related to race, diversity, inclusion and differences of all kinds.
   ❑ 1　　　❑ 2　　　❑ 3　　　❑ 4　　　❑ 5

5. Discussions in this group have helped me see the value of my work with families.
   ❑ 1　　　❑ 2　　　❑ 3　　　❑ 4　　　❑ 5

6. In this group I feel seen and valued even when I express something that is unusual or differs from the majority.
   ❑ 1　　　❑ 2　　　❑ 3　　　❑ 4　　　❑ 5

7. Discussions in this group have helped me see the perspectives of people who are different from me in terms of race, culture, religion, or approach to my work.
   ❑ 1　　　❑ 2　　　❑ 3　　　❑ 4　　　❑ 5

8. In this group I have gathered ideas and insights that have helped me do my work in more effective ways.
   ❑ 1　　　❑ 2　　　❑ 3　　　❑ 4　　　❑ 5

9. When I leave this group I feel supported and refreshed.
   ❑ 1　　　❑ 2　　　❑ 3　　　❑ 4　　　❑ 5

10. I would recommend groups like this to others doing work like mine.
    ❑ 1　　　❑ 2　　　❑ 3　　　❑ 4　　　❑ 5

It is possible to track these questions after each session using a platform such as Survey Monkey noting changes in the ratings or to use at the beginning and ending of a series of sessions.

APPENDIX 9

Measuring Reflective Supervision within Home Visiting

Here are some examples of evaluation instruments which have been used to study various aspects of reflective practice and supervision.

- **The ProQOL (Professional Quality of Life)** has been used to measure compassion satisfaction in those receiving reflective practice to support their work. ***https://proqol.org***

- **Burnout, A Review of Theory and Measurement.** ***https://www.ncbi.nlm.nih.gov/pmc/articles/PMC8834764***

- **Measuring Reflective Supervision Within Home Visiting: Changes in Supervisor's Self-perception Over Time.** This article discusses the properties of four widely used assessments of reflective supervisors self-perception over time examining their usefulness as evaluation tools. Low, C. M., Newland, R., Silver, R. B., Parade, S., Remington, S., Aguiar, S., & Campagna, K. (2018). Infant Mental Health Journal, 39(5), 608–617.

- **Infant mental health home visiting therapists' reflective supervision self-efficacy in community practice settings** Sarah E. Shea,Jennifer M. Jester,Alissa C. Huth-Bocks,Deborah J. Weatherston,Maria Muzik,Katherine L. Rosenblum,The Michigan Collaborative for Infant Mental Health Research, 2019. ***https://doi.org/10.1002/imhj.21834***

- **The Reflective Supervision Self-Efficacy Scale for Supervisees (RSSESS)** is a self-report measure that has been used in previous evaluations and is designed to assess perceived reflective practice self-efficacy for Infant Mental Health-Home Visiting (IMH-HV) therapists. The RSSESS is a reliable tool to measure change in reflective practice skills. IMH-HV therapists demonstrated growth in their use of reflective practice skills with families and their observational skills over the 12-month period. In addition, results indicated correlations between reflective supervision self-efficacy and job satisfaction as well as burnout.

- **Development of the reflective practice questionnaire: preliminary findings.** Priddis, Lynn & Rogers, Shane. (2018). Reflective Practice. 19. 1-16. ***https://www.tandfonline.com/doi/full/10.1080/146239 43.2017.1379384***

RUPTURE & REPAIR FRAMEWORK

HOW IT

SHOULD & SHOULDN'T

BE USED

There are several ways that the framework can be used to foster repair and if used incorrectly or with the wrong purpose it can create space for harm to occur. Review this document with all parties prior to employing the framework.

Thoughtful Connection & Repair

Organizations should utilize the framework to take individuals and groups through a thoughtful process not dictated by time limits but by individual readiness. The process should honor each person's needs to ensure a healthy and authentic repair.

Checklist

All those engaging in the repair process **should not** do so with speed or the intent of rapidly completing a step in order to move to the next step. This framework is designed for intentional reflection; authentic conversation; and provides the ability to revisit steps as needed.

Self-Reflection

Use the framework for personal and professional growth. Take time to review the reflection questions with the understanding that some responses will come naturally, and others may require space for researching, learning, and reflecting.

Create Trust

The repair process may deepen existing trust. However, a degree of trust amongst those utilizing the framework needs to exist before engaging in the repair process. Individuals **should not** use the framework to force someone into a trusting relationship. The process is voluntary for each step to honor those who may want to use a different method for repair and for relationships where trust has not been established.

Adaptation

Organizations can adapt the framework to meet their unique needs and challenges. Remember that the framework is not a solution for all challenges and ruptures, and adaptation and use should be a collective decision made by all parties involved in the rupture and repair process.

Punitive

Information shared during the rupture and repair process **should not** be utilized for retaliation, as a reference in performance reviews, or to hold individuals accountable for concerns that are not part of the rupture. This framework is solely to repair valued relationships, and if misused as a punitive measure, there will be no repair.

For additional information or assistance with the Rupture & Repair Process contact info@mycolabpartners.com

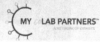

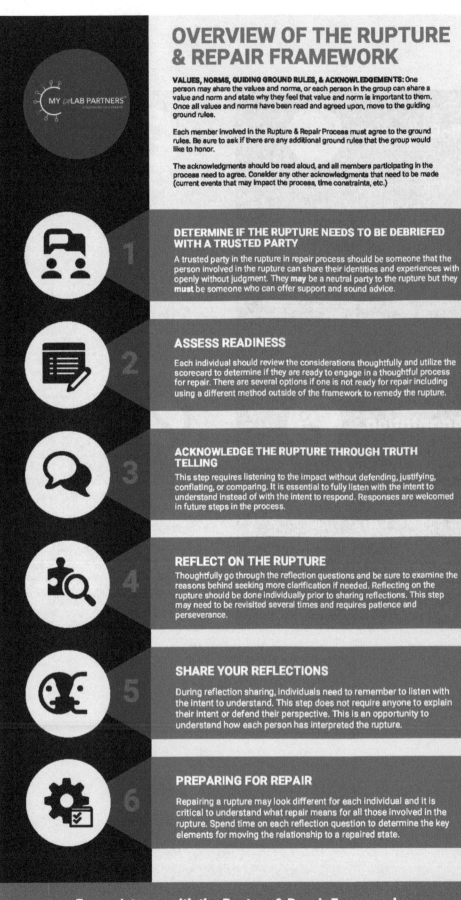

OVERVIEW OF THE RUPTURE & REPAIR FRAMEWORK

VALUES, NORMS, GUIDING GROUND RULES, & ACKNOWLEDGEMENTS: One person may share the values and norms, or each person in the group can share a value and norm and state why they feel that value and norm is important to them. Once all values and norms have been read and agreed upon, move to the guiding ground rules.

Each member involved in the Rupture & Repair Process must agree to the ground rules. Be sure to ask if there are any additional ground rules that the group would like to honor.

The acknowledgments should be read aloud, and all members participating in the process need to agree. Consider any other acknowledgments that need to be made (current events that may impact the process, time constraints, etc.)

1 DETERMINE IF THE RUPTURE NEEDS TO BE DEBRIEFED WITH A TRUSTED PARTY

A trusted party in the rupture in repair process should be someone that the person involved in the rupture can share their identities and experiences with openly without judgment. They **may** be a neutral party to the rupture but they **must** be someone who can offer support and sound advice.

2 ASSESS READINESS

Each individual should review the considerations thoughtfully and utilize the scorecard to determine if they are ready to engage in a thoughtful process for repair. There are several options if one is not ready for repair including using a different method outside of the framework to remedy the rupture.

3 ACKNOWLEDGE THE RUPTURE THROUGH TRUTH TELLING

This step requires listening to the impact without defending, justifying, conflating, or comparing. It is essential to fully listen with the intent to understand instead of with the intent to respond. Responses are welcomed in future steps in the process.

4 REFLECT ON THE RUPTURE

Thoughtfully go through the reflection questions and be sure to examine the reasons behind seeking more clarification if needed. Reflecting on the rupture should be done individually prior to sharing reflections. This step may need to be revisited several times and requires patience and perseverance.

5 SHARE YOUR REFLECTIONS

During reflection sharing, individuals need to remember to listen with the intent to understand. This step does not require anyone to explain their intent or defend their perspective. This is an opportunity to understand how each person has interpreted the rupture.

6 PREPARING FOR REPAIR

Repairing a rupture may look different for each individual and it is critical to understand what repair means for all those involved in the rupture. Spend time on each reflection question to determine the key elements for moving the relationship to a repaired state.

For assistance with the Rupture & Repair Framework contact info@mycolabpartners.com

OVERVIEW OF THE RUPTURE & REPAIR FRAMEWORK

VALUES, NORMS, GUIDING GROUND RULES, & ACKNOWLEDGEMENTS SHOULD BE REVISITED DURING STEPS 7-12.

7 ACHIEVING LOGISTICAL AGREEMENT

The rupture and repair process should be inclusive, and repair should take place in an environment that eliminates bias, favoritism, and discomfort to the extent possible. Therefore, all parties must agree on how the repair process will be convened. There needs to be agreement on the neutral party to ensure neutrality (this may also be an outside entity that assists in repair.) The trusted party is only considered neutral if they were sought out by all individuals involved and agreed that they can be impartial.

8 START THE REPAIR PROCESS

Restating ground rules and acknowledgments is essential before starting the repair process. This step may require multiple conversations and should go at the pace necessary for all those involved. Referring to previous reflections and sharing is advised during this step to ensure clarity and thoughtfulness.

9 SEEK OUT COMMON GROUND

There may not be an agreement in all areas of the rupture and the repair, but it is vital to share the areas where there is a shared understanding. Use the opportunity to focus on the importance of the rupture, the outcome, and the commitment to change.

10 PLAN A PATH FORWARD

Collectively plan a path forward that can be shared with others while also honoring confidentiality. This step is for fruitful discussion, and those involved must keep in mind that some may want to take time to review and reflect on the questions individually before collaborative planning.

11 FOLLOW-UP ON THE REPAIR

After 30 days, the path forward for repair should be reviewed by all involved to assess progress, discuss challenges, and any needed adjustments. Be willing to revisit steps, make new considerations, or listen to new requests to ensure repair has or can be achieved.

12 COMMIT TO LIFELONG LEARNING

Commit to continuing to learn about self and others to prevent future repairs and be better prepared for when other ruptures occur.

For assistance with the Rupture & Repair Framework contact info@mycolabpartners.com

MY CoLAB PARTNERS
A DIVISION OF [illegible]

RUPTURE & REPAIR FRAMEWORK

The Rupture & Repair Framework guides groups and individuals to address and repair ruptures through a thoughtful process. Before starting the process, each person must review and explicitly agree to the values and norms, guiding ground rules, and acknowledgments. All steps in the process can and should be revisited as needed.

① VALUES & NORMS

We confront White supremacy.
- We name and confront White supremacy & systemic oppression in ourselves, our organization & our sector. We do this as a means of promoting equity and working in a just relationship with one another.

We value multiple perspectives.
- We respect and seek out multiple opinions, experiences, and learning styles. We are committed listeners, and we invest the time in listening to understand instead of listening to respond. We are committed to making inclusive decisions and restoring relationships that have experienced rupture.

We get brave and specific.
- We support one another to be brave and specific so that we can resolve issues and overcome barriers to equitable collaboration. We do this by speaking our truths without fear of retaliation because all perspectives are seen as a means to advance the conversation.

We seek to learn together.
- We learn together to generate new, innovative possibilities. We accept that mistakes are part of the learning process, and we support one another in taking risks.

We are willing to get comfortable with discomfort.
- We recognize that with discomfort, there is growth. Therefore, we accept the discomfort of exploring challenging topics and will strive not to cause harm in discomfort.

② GUIDING GROUND RULES

Listen to Understand
- We agree to truly listen to what people are saying with the intent to understand vs. the intent to respond.

Respectful Talking
- We agree not to talk over anyone, ensure voices who experience multiple forms of privilege are not dominating conversations, and avoid sidebar conversations.

"I" not "You" Statements
- We agree to not attribute our feelings to other people by intentionally using I statements – "I think, I feel, I know, or I believe."

Respect different opinions, experiences, and perspectives
- We agree to reflect on the knowledge that each person comes to the discussion from different viewpoints and experiences. Reaching a consensus or agreement may not be feasible or the intended outcome.

Retaliation is Unacceptable
- We agree to not use this framework as a means of retaliation, as punitive measures, or as a reference of performance.

③ ACKNOWLEDGEMENTS

We acknowledge that repairing ruptures requires us to be lifelong learners. Regardless of titles or expertise, we will approach each discussion and experience open to learning and expect that our learning will continue beyond today.

We acknowledge that we not only need safe spaces but brave spaces. This means saying what we truly feel and think without fear of retaliation and being unafraid to listen to the impact on others. It also means that we need to be brave enough to stay in the conversation and be open to being changed.

We acknowledge and accept non-closure in the first engagement. This is important as we do not want to rush to solutions for the benefit of comfort but want to be thoughtful in the process to safeguard authenticity and learning. This also means that steps may be revisited before moving forward.

We acknowledge that repairing ruptures requires holding space for <u>Powerful Groups Targeted for Oppression (PGTOs)</u> to lead, identify needed resources and solutions.

We acknowledge that it may not be safe to resolve conflicts alone and are open to involving others (external facilitators, others who experienced or witnessed the harm, support for PGTOs, etc.) to listen and help with the process.

We acknowledge that participating in the repair process must be voluntary, and we will not attempt to force either party to participate in an unwanted process.

RUPTURE & REPAIR PROCESS

The Rupture & Repair Process gives the person(s) who have been harmed an opportunity to communicate with those who have caused harm to share the real impact of the harm. It also holds people who have caused the harm accountable for what they have done and helps them take responsibility and begin repairing the rupture. Keep in mind that some ruptures will evoke an immediate response, while other ruptures may sit with those harmed for some time before being able to share and engage in the process. **The Rupture & Repair Process requires more than one conversation.** The first conversation should solely be for listening and reflecting. Follow-up conversations should seek to achieve shared understanding.

When Ruptures Occur in the Moment:

Interrupt the rupture by doing one of the following:
- Expressing how you feel in the moment (e.g., *"I am feeling furious, uncomfortable and unsafe by what is happening."*)

- Expressing what is needed (e.g., *"Could we take 10 minutes and come back to this?"*)

- Expressing your desire to engage in the Rupture & Repair Process (e.g., *"I think/know a rupture is occurring, and I would like to address this using our committed process."*)

Our Committed Process

1 **Determine if the rupture needs to be debriefed with a trusted party** before engaging those who caused harm. Suppose a trusted party is required, be sure to share why you are requesting their support using the consideration(s) that resonates with you or the group.

Considerations:

○ If I am not a member of the group who experiences privilege (e.g., white, male, heterosexual, positional power, etc.) does the power and privilege of those who will be part of the process concern me? **If yes,** debrief with a trusted party and consider requesting a neutral party to assist with the process.

○ Do I/we feel safe to address the harm? **If not,** consider discussing with a trusted party.

○ Is there pressure from specific individuals or groups to engage in this dialogue? **If yes,** debrief with a trusted party

○ Is there concern that the other person or group will not understand why this is a rupture? **If yes,** debrief with a trusted party and consider requesting a neutral party to assist with the process.

○ Is there a concern that another conflict will arise from addressing the rupture? **If yes,** debrief with a trusted party.

○ Are there past harms that feel unresolved with the group or individual? **If yes,** debrief with a trusted party.

Ready for Step 2?

RUPTURE & REPAIR PROCESS

2 **Assess readiness for engaging in the process.** Readiness can take time because it requires you to reflect on assumptions, fears, and awareness of yourself and others. Do not rush through this phase for the sake of creating comfort and arriving at a solution. If you are not ready to move forward, communicate that with others and explore ways to prepare for a thoughtful process.

Considerations:

○ What power (positional, knowledge, experience, associated with privilege, etc.) do I have in the situation?

○ What influence do I have over the outcomes?

○ Do I have an understanding of my biases?

○ Do I know the history of the other group(s) from their perspective and the history within my own group(s)?

○ Do I understand the underlying systems that impact outcomes for the group?

○ Am I aware of various communication and conflict styles (emotional restraint vs. emotional expressiveness, discussion style, engagement style, accommodation style, dynamic style, direct vs. indirect, etc.)?

○ Are there past harms that will impact my engagement in the process?

○ What assumptions do I have?

○ Am I aware that there are differences that make a difference in experiences?

○ What is needed for me to engage in the Rupture & Repair Process authentically?

Readiness Scorecard	Strongly Agree (5)	Agree (4)	Neither Agree or Disagree (3)	Disagree (2)	Strongly Disagree (1)
I am aware of the power I have in the situation					
I am aware of the level of influence I have over the outcome					
I have done the work to understand my biases					
I understand the history of other groups from their perspective and the history within my own groups.					
I am informed about the underlying systems that impact outcomes for the group(s)					
I am aware of different communication styles					
I have addressed past harms with those who I am going through the process with					
I have noted any assumptions I have about the rupture that has occurred					
I am aware that differences make a difference in experiences					
I have identified what is needed for me to authentically engage and have taken steps to share those needs with a trusted party					
I am committed to our values, norms, ground rules, and acknowledgements					
Total Score Per Column					

Total Readiness Score: ☐

If your score is **below 38 and you are the party who caused harm**, request more time in Step 4 of the process to get assistance with readiness.
If your score is **below 38 and you are the receiver of harm**, request assistance from a trusted individual to explore your readiness score before moving to Step 3.

Above 38, Move to Step 3 ⤵

RUPTURE & REPAIR PROCESS

3 **Acknowledge the rupture through truth-telling.**
This step focuses on listening to the impact and **not conveying intent, defending, or justifying actions.**

Reflect on the ground rule of listening to understand as there will be future opportunities to ask clarifying questions. Remember, as someone shares, there is diversity in communication styles. Some may convey emotions, while others may hold back and focus solely on concrete facts. Either way, both are equally important to gain clarity on impact.

Bring all impacted members and any needed and agreed upon trusted individuals , and an agreed upon neutral party together to understand the impact of the rupture from all viewpoints.

- If the **party that caused harm** starts the conversation, they should lead with questions (e.g., "What did I do to harm you/the group/the process?").

- If the **receiver(s) of harm** starts the conversation, be sure to highlight behaviors, actions, decisions, and any language that has contributed to the harm. This approach will assist in Step 4, focused on reflection.

Be mindful as the listener to those who have been harmed not to conflate, compare, or contrast. We must listen to others with an open mind, hearing their story without injecting ourselves into it, making listening to those impacted the top priority. A useful practice after someone has shared, and it has resonated with you is to respond with "Heard."

Values, Ground Rules, and Acknowledgements to Keep in Mind:

- We value multiple perspectives.

- We get brave and specific.

- We seek to learn together.

- We are willing to get comfortable with discomfort.

- Listen to Understand

- Respectful Talking

- "I" not "You" Statements

- We acknowledge that repairing ruptures requires us to be lifelong learners.

- We acknowledge that we not only need safe spaces but brave spaces.

- We acknowledge that repairing ruptures requires us to hold space for Powerful

  Groups Targeted for Oppression (PGTOs)

Ready for Step 4?

4 **Reflect on the rupture.** Each person involved in the rupture should participate in reflection. Those harmed by the rupture should share their reflections with a trusted party or group. Those who enacted the rupture should also share their reflections with a trusted party or group. Allow for individuals to reflect on the rupture for a **minimum of 24 hours.**

Questions for reflection:

1. How did I feel about the conversation?

2. What biases may have contributed to the rupture?

3. What did I learn, and what resonated with me?

4. What was challenging to hear and why?

5. Did anything surprise me, and why?

6. What role did I play in the rupture? (caused harm, a contributor to harm, a receiver of rupture, a silent party, an observer, an interrupter, an accomplice, etc.)

7. What could have been done differently?

8. What else do I need to learn about or get clarification on before I have the following conversation?

Ready for Step 5?

RUPTURE & REPAIR PROCESS

5 **Share your reflections of the rupture.** This step is solely for listening and does not require either group to defend their perspectives or explain intent. This step is for gaining perspective and a greater understanding of impact. *Remember, you do not have to come to an agreement, just an understanding.*

Steps to Follow:

1. Have those who caused harm to acknowledge what was shared with them

2. The person who caused harm can share their reflections or may ask for more reflection time.

3. Both parties may ask clarifying open-ended questions.

4. Both parties should acknowledge what has been shared.

5. State any areas of common ground that were shared (e.g., "I can appreciate that we both felt/experienced/belive/were surprised..." "I noticed that there seems to be a shared understanding around...").

6. Ask if each person involved is ready to move to Step 6 as **there must be consensus before proceeding to Step 6.**

7. If there **isn't consensus, revisit Step 4** until all involved do not have any clarifying questions.

Checking for Consensus:

Each person must select 4 or above to move to Step 6.

1. I fully support and am ready to move to the space of repairing this rupture.

2. I have some minor concerns that I want to reflect on, but I am okay with moving to the repair process.

3. I can move forward with the repair process, but I have some reservations that may require more reflection time and an opportunity to share if I find they are not resolved during the repair.

4. I am not okay with moving forward and will only be an observer in the repair process as I do not want to prevent others from repairing the rupture *(Only Applies to Group Ruptures).*

5. I am not ready to move to the repair process, nor will I participate in the repair process, but I am okay if others in the group move forward without me *(Only Applies to Group Ruptures).*

6. I am not ready for the repair process and need more time for reflection and sharing.

7. I do not want to engage in the repair process, and I want to consider another approach for this rupture.

Ready for Step 6?

RUPTURE & REPAIR PROCESS

6 **Preparing for repair .** During this step, each person is taking time to identify key elements needed for an authentic repair.

Questions for reflection:

1. **Why is this an important conversation to have? (consider the impact to you, the group, the organization, and the work)**

2. **What are you hoping will be achieved by addressing the rupture for you, the group, other stakeholders/communities, the organization, and the work?**

3. **What do you want to be different after the repair process?**

4. **What do you believe is needed to repair and reset the relationship (shared understanding, policies, new practices, apology with a stated action, etc.)?**

Trending needs for repairing conflict:
- Empathy
- Openness
- Time
- Honesty
- Direct feedback
- Not being defined by a mistake
- Everyone has a voice
- Recognizing there is not only one right answer
- Transparency
- Accountability
- Commitment
- Compassion
- Understanding
- Collaboration
- Goals
- Action

7 **Achieving logistical agreement.** There must be agreement on all logistical components.

Logistical Considerations	Suggestions with Rationale	Agreement (Y/N)
Will this be a group conversation or a one-on-one conversation?		
Who will convene and facilitate the dialogue (DEI Team, affinity group, neutral party, external party), and what is the rationale (mitigate power dynamics, neutrality, perspectives, etc.) for the selected individual(s)?		
How will you convene the repair process (virtually, in-person, or a combination)?		
How many sessions do you believe are needed for repair?		
When should the repair process begin? (consider the time needed for readiness and reflection)		

Ready for Step 8?

RUPTURE & REPAIR PROCESS

8 **Start the repair process.** Remember to honor the ground rule of using "I" vs. "You" statements, and be sure to attack the rupture and not the person. Consider that the repair process may require several conversations and may not get resolved in one encounter.

Steps to Follow:

1. Have **each person** share their "why" from Step 6

2. Those **who are harmed** will share what they hope is achieved by addressing the rupture.

3. Those **who caused harm** should use this opportunity to own their role in the rupture and any new perspectives gained through reflection.

4. **Each person involved** should share what they want to be different and how they believe that can be achieved.

5. **Those harmed** will share what is needed to repair and reset the relationship (shared understanding, policies, new practices, apology with a stated action, etc.)?

6. Those **who caused harm** will take accountability by discussing how the needs expressed can be met and commit to generating change.

7. **The group** will discuss what loving accountability will take place to foster repaired relationships.

8. **The group** will discuss what needs to change to prevent similar ruptures from occurring again. Be sure to center PGTOs in the discussion.

Are You Ready to Seek Out Common Ground?

Do I realize ruptures can be complex and not easily resolved?

What energy do I have to expend to learn more about the other perspective?

Am I willing to put in the time it will take?

Am I willing to engage in teachable moments?

9 **Seek out common ground. Identify areas of agreement and understanding.**

- Focus on what is most important about the rupture.

- Consider why a specific outcome is important to all parties.

- Recognize shared commitment to results and not just solutions

- Appreciate agreement on how someone wants be held accountable

Ready for Step 10?

RUPTURE & REPAIR PROCESS

10 **Plan a path forward.** To reduce the likelihood of repeating the rupture it is vital to implement a plan of action and share that plan with others who may not have been aware of the rupture for learning and accountability while honoring confidentiality. The considerations below should be reviewed and discussed collectively with all parties involved in the rupture.

Considerations:

1. List the agreed upon desired results

2. What policies or practices need to change to honor the repair and how will that change happen?

3. What other identities need to be considered to prevent repeating the rupture?

4. What measures are in place for loving accountability while working to achieve desired results?

5. Are there any solutions that were provided in the repair that can be applied to other areas of the work, group, or the organization?

7. How frequently will you check-in on the repair and the progress made?

8. How will you communicate barriers encountered while seeking to repair the rupture?

9. What indicators will determine if the repair has been achieved?

Ready for Step 11?

RUPTURE & REPAIR PROCESS

11 **Follow-up on the repair.** Checking in during and after the repair is key. It shows genuine care and provides an opportunity for those involved in the repair process to share success and challenges after an agreement was reached. Additionally, this gives participants a chance to troubleshoot and share lessons learned. **Follow-up should take place no sooner than 30 days.**

Considerations during the follow-up:

- Do the agreements made need fine-tuning due to lived experiences or unforeseen challenges?

- What aspects of the agreement have been working well?

- What has been done differently since the agreement (policies, practices, communication, accountability)?

- What aspects of the agreement have been challenging/frustrating/disappointing?

- Are there any steps in the process that you feel should be revisited?

- Have you shared success and challenges with others to foster continued learning?

12 **Commit to lifelong learning.**

- I commit to learning ways to be intentionally inclusive.

- I commit to taking the time to understand myself in order to better understand others.

- I commit to exposing myself to difference and I acknowledge that I don't know what I don't know but will not use what is unconscious as an excuse.

- I commit to speaking up and speaking out even when I am not directly impacted because I understand there is no neutrality when it comes to achieving equity.

- I commit to being curious and not judgmental, pausing and listening, getting comfortable with discomfort, and calling out power dynamics that can get in the way of growth and community.

- I commit to doing better when I know better and reminding myself that equity is a journey not a destination.

 *For additional information or assistance with the Rupture & Repair Process contact info@mycolabpartners.com*

ONLINE RESOURCES – LINKS MADE EASY

Section 1 – Online Resource Easy Links

 Reflective Supervision: What We Know and What We Need to Know to Support and Strengthen the Home Visiting Workforce. (ACF, DHHS)

 Using Reflective Supervision to Support Trauma-Informed Systems for Children (Multiplying Connections)

 Status of the Evidence for Infant and Early Childhood Mental Health Consultation (iecmh.org)

 Secondary Traumatic Stress Core Competencies for Trauma INformed Support and Supervision: Cross Disciplinary Version.

 Can Preschool Expulsion Be Prevented?

 Early Childhood Mental Health Consultation: Results of a Statewide Random-Controlled Evaluation.

Section 2 – Online Resource Easy Links

 https://closecollaboration.utu.fi/eng/2019/08/27/reflective-group-supervision-and-some-guidelines/

 Demystifying Reflective Practice

 Georgetown University's Center of Excellence for Early Childhood Mental Health Consultation to Infant and Early Childhood Programs.

 Center of Excellence for Infant and Early Childhood Mental Health Consultation | SAMHSA

 The Reflective Case Discussion Model of Group Supervision

Section 3 – Online Resource Easy Links

 Facilitation Tips | Reflective Practice Facilitator tips

 13.1 Understanding Small Groups – Communication in the Real World

 Groupthink | Understanding the Impact of Group Dynamics in Decision Making

 Mindfulness Exercises

 A 12-Minute Medication for Challenging Emotions

 21 Mindfulness Exercises & Activities For Adults (+ PDF)

 Mindfulness for Racial Justice | Taking Charge of Your Health & Wellbeing

 Tool: Interrupting Microaggressions

 How Microaggressions are Like Mosquito Bites • Same Difference

 Racial Healing Self-Care Mindfulness Exercise

Made in United States
Orlando, FL
02 August 2024

49866627R00057